"My World Is Gone"

"My World Is Gone"

memories of life
in a **southern**
cotton mill town

George G. Suggs, Jr.

WAYNE STATE UNIVERSITY PRESS   DETROIT

Suggs, George G., 1929–
"My world is gone" : memories of life in a
southern cotton mill town / George C. Suggs.
p. cm.
Includes bibliographical references and index.
ISBN 0-8143-3035-5
1. Suggs, George G., 1929– 2. Textile workers—North
Carolina—Bladenboro—Biography. 3. Cotton textile
industry—North Carolina—Bladenboro—History. I. Title.
HD8039.T42 U6684 2002
331.7'677'0975632—dc21   2001006561

For Dad and the workers of the Bladenboro Cotton Mills
and to the memory of my mother, Carrie E. Suggs

Contents

Contents

Illustrations

Acknowledgments

Several individuals were unusually helpful in preparing the pictorial section of this volume. William Butler, Sam Pait, and Mack Hester of the Bladenboro Historical Museum made themselves available at inconvenient times to allow my selection and reproduction of photographs from the museum. Dewey Bridger, son of Dr. Dewey H. Bridger, graciously provided a picture of his father. John Lee Hammond, former hard-hitting third baseman of the Bladenboro Spinners Ball Club, supplied a picture of the team. Ewen Hester provided a picture of his grandfather Alfie Davis. Michael Simmons, editor of the *Bladen Journal,* granted permission to use a picture of workers in the Bladenboro Cotton Mills first published in his *Southeastern Times.* And Marie Wilson Phinney, daughter of Graham and Ada Wilson, made available a picture of White Oak Original Free Will Baptist Church. I am indebted to all of them for their help.

This work is rooted in memory and recollection fed and refreshed over the years by numerous conversations with my parents; my brother, Charles; my aunts, uncles, cousins; and my friends—all of whom kept the past alive. I am immensely grateful to all of them. Unfortunately, most of them are deceased. At the time of this writing, however, my father, whose "gone" world is the principal subject of this volume, remains alive with a mind that is remarkable for its clarity and grasp of the past. His mill years remain vibrant in memory. When I needed confirmation of a personal memory concerning a person or event, I consulted him. Nevertheless, I am fully responsible for whatever errors appear in this volume.

Finally, to my wife, Virginia, I offer my deepest appreciation for her sacrifices and strong encouragement over the years. She has helped to make my professional journey from "there" to "here" much less difficult. This book would not have been possible without her loving support.

Introduction

A Lost World

When my father was in his early eighties, he and I visited the site where once had stood the Old Mill village of the Bladenboro Cotton Mills. The village—commonly known as the Old Mill "hill"—was the first of two the company built to house workers for the mills it constructed in 1912 and 1916. The two mills were locally called the Old Mill. A third mill, called the New Mill, was built in 1923. It had a smaller village that residents called the New Mill "hill." For more than half a century, these two villages, each containing dozens of company-owned houses and separated from each other by the Butler Mill branch, were home to hundreds of mill hands and their families. Today they no longer exist.

The two village sites are now occupied by modern subsidized housing that contains far more conveniences than had the basic company housing that once stood there. But at the time of our nostalgic return to the site of the Old Mill village, it was gradually being reclaimed by weeds, brush, and trees. Other than the faint traces of the village streets, there was little else to suggest that for years a thriving, organized community of working families had occupied this place.

Located a short distance west of the town of Bladenboro, North Carolina, and parallel to Highway 211 and the Seaboard Airline Railway, Bladenboro Cotton Mills and their villages once formed an island of industrialization that challenged the prevailing agrarian culture based on the production of tobacco, cotton, peanuts, corn, and forest products such as turpentine, tar, and lumber. Like a number of mills located in Lumberton, St. Pauls, Rockingham, Wilmington, Hope Mills, and elsewhere in the region, Bladenboro Cotton Mills was essentially a family-owned business. It was founded by R. L. and H. C. Bridger, two brothers who left

Little River, South Carolina, in 1885 to settle in the unincorporated town of Bladenboro.

Before the arrival of the Bridgers, the principal occupations of the people living in the southern part of Bladen County were farming and harvesting turpentine, tar, and lumber from the surrounding forests. During the next quarter-century, the Bridger brothers actively engaged in these enterprises while increasing their landholdings. They also expanded into the mercantile business, which they eventually incorporated as the Bridger Corporation. So prosperous was this enterprise that by 1911 they found it necessary to build a much larger brick structure to house and facilitate their growing business. The brothers gradually became the driving force in the local economy.

While doing so, they set the stage for the next generation of

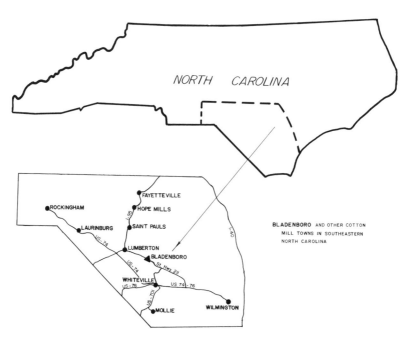

Map showing Bladenboro and other cotton mill towns in southeastern North Carolina. Courtesy of the author.

family members to expand the Bridger interests into other enterprises such as cotton ginning and banking. In 1908 they established the Bank of Bladenboro, an institution that remained a family concern for eighty-six years—even throughout the Great Depression of the thirties—until it was sold in 1994. However, the Bridgers's largest and most important enterprise was Bladenboro Cotton Mills, whose first two mills (the Old Mill) were constructed in 1912 and 1916 to produce yarn. The Old Mill and the New Mill, built in 1923, continued to operate until they were sold in 1980. For years the company was the largest employer in Bladen County.

When construction began on the Old Mill, my father was a boy of seven. Born in 1905 on a small farm near Mollie in Columbus County, North Carolina, he was the youngest of six boys and three girls. He and his family were to became part of

The Bladenboro Cotton Mills in the mid-fifties. The Old Mill with its village and the company store are located in the center and lower right, and the New Mill and its village are situated to the left of center.
Courtesy of Bladenboro Historical Museum.

the movement of similar families from the farm to the cotton mills when persuasive recruiters began scouring the countryside for "hands" to work in new factories like the newly organized Bladenboro Cotton Mills. His personal odyssey began in the fall of 1916, when two of his older brothers, enticed by friends, left the farm to take jobs in the cotton mills of East Lumberton in nearby Robeson County. (Lumberton then had mills in both the east and west sections of the city.) In time the entire family moved to East Lumberton, attracted there by a recruiter's promise of good housing, a no-expense move, and jobs for family members. It was there that my father, a boy of eleven, and his brothers, still in their early teens, were introduced into the mills.

During the next six years, the family was nomadic, moving among the many small mill towns that had been constructed in southeastern North Carolina. East Lumberton, Rockingham, Wilmington, Hope Mills, St. Pauls—all had a mill or mills whose management was eager to attract large families like my father's. His family worked in all of them. It was not until 1923 that his family finally settled permanently in Bladenboro. However, my father—now eighteen and on his own—continued to move among the many cotton mills in the area, most of which were family-owned like Bladenboro Cotton Mills. He experienced little difficulty in finding work. Having worked in the mills since age eleven, he had mastered a variety of mill jobs. His skills combined with the high demand for labor made possible his frequent moves from mill to mill. Between 1923 and his marriage in 1927, he worked in the Great Falls Mill in Rockingham, leaving there for a mill in St. Pauls, returning to Rockingham to work in the Hannah-Pickett Mill, moving again to the mill in St. Pauls and, finally, after briefly working for the Carolina Power and Light Company, settling in Bladenboro to work in the Bladenboro Cotton Mills.

After their marriage in 1927, he and my mother took up residence in the Old Mill village. Unaccustomed to the close living that village life entailed, my mother (whose father was a small sawmill entrepreneur who had helped to supply the lumber to construct the Old Mill with its village) did not like village living. Once the family shared a four-room house with my father's sister Clara and her husband; later they shared a similar house with my mother's sister Marybelle and her family of three; and lastly they shared a four-room house with my mother's Uncle Seth and his family of four. Living in such close quarters generated enormous stress. Although it meant leaving behind many of her relatives who lived in the village, my mother longed to own her own home in less stressful surroundings. Consequently, between 1927 and the fall of 1937, the family "escaped" the village three times for short periods, only to be driven back by financial necessity to live in one of the company's rented houses. Not until 1937 was the family able to make a permanent break from the Old Mill village and live in a very modest home south of town.

Born in the Old Mill village in 1929, I knew little about our

The author and his parents, George G. and Carrie E. Suggs, standing in front of their company house in the Old Mill village (c. 1933). Courtesy of George G. Suggs, Sr.

family's first departure and return there in late 1931 to share a house with my mother's sister Marybelle and her family. But the childhood years between then and our leaving again in 1934 were very impressionable years that were marked by a growing knowledge of neighbors, relatives, and the flow of life of the village. On our unpaved street with its unpainted, L-shaped houses and outhouses, I learned who lived where—neighbors like the Deavers, Ludlums, Singletarys, Williams, Tylers, Paits, Jacksons, and the Taylors. I knew about the company store, what was sold there and who worked there—Emmett Guyton, the manager; Ruby Dunn, a clerk who ran the soda fountain; Miller Bridger and Margaret (Maggie) Bridger, office managers; Coy Hickman and Waitus Edwards, meat cutters. I observed how blasts from the shift whistle regulated the lives of hundreds of workers who walked the dirt sidewalks to and from their work in the mills. I watched and listened to workers as they discussed conditions in the mills, the town, the state, and the country—sometimes on porches of nearby relatives on Sunday afternoons or at the end of the Old Mill where they had gathered—as they sat smoking, chewing tobacco, dipping snuff, and whittling as they whiled the time away. I observed how villagers responded to tragedy and death. When we left the Old Mill village in late 1934, it was to be, my mother thought, for the last time. It wasn't.

In the spring of 1937 we returned again to the Old Mill village after stints of living on my grandfather's farm north of town, in my Uncle Artie's house in Bladenboro, and in a simple shotgun house that my father had partially built with used lumber on Pine Ridge west of the New Mill. The birth of my brother, Charles, increased the family to four, making it too large for the unfinished house. Once again the family temporarily returned to the Old Mill village to live in two rooms of a four-room house then occupied by my mother's Uncle Seth Hester and his family of four. Across the street living in similar quarters were my father's sister Clara and her husband, who shared a house with a family of Taylors. We remained in this different section of the village until the summer of 1938, when again we moved into a small house built by my father south of town on the Whiteville road. However, we had remained in the village long enough for me to become acquainted with even more families whose company houses were clustered near ours. Although my father continued to work in the mills until 1942, when he found employment in the shipyard of Wilmington during World War II, the family never again lived in housing of the Bladenboro Cotton Mills.

However, with relatives still resident there, we were frequently in and out of the villages. And after the war, when the shipyard ceased operations, my father was forced again to seek employment in the mills, where he found again many of the men he had worked with in past years. Furthermore, many relatives and others who worked in the mills were fellow members of the White Oak Original Free Will Baptist Church, a working-class church whose members consisted principally of mill employees. As a result, he found it easy to maintain contact with men and women who had shared his earlier working years as a mill hand. Through the years he continued to cultivate these associations, even after he left the mills again for work in the shipyard at Newport News, Virginia. The same was true in his years of retirement. He valued the friendship of fellow mill workers.

Unfortunately, when we visited the former site of the Old Mill village, too many of the people who had resided there in the dozens of company houses had died. Just as the houses in the villages had disappeared one by one following the decision of management to rid the company of these diminished assets by giving them away, former longtime employees had disappeared one by one as they fell victim to illnesses and old age. With their passage, the world that my father had known—the villages, the untold number of fellow workers—had also gradually slipped away.

As we walked about the site where the Old Mill village once had stood, we talked about his lost world. Although in his eighties and with faint visual evidence to rely on, he nevertheless easily reconstructed the layout of the village. He remembered the unnamed streets; the locations of houses where our family and others whom he had known had lived; episodes in the lives of men with whom he had worked, men like John Pait, Tulley Singletary, Lon Deaver, David James Pait, Bill Hester, Fred Williams, Jetter Hester, Leland Shipman, Bob Hester, Jim Hester, and many others; and the hard times of the thirties, when the Depression made life so difficult. He talked about these things as we stopped and paused at familiar home sites of people we had known. When it came time to leave, he turned to me and said sadly: "You know, my world is gone." There was nothing I could do but agree with him.

It was this visit to the site of the Old Mill village of the Bladenboro Cotton Mills that prompted this book. Possessing many sessions of tape-recorded conversations with my father, I used them to inform and confirm my youthful memories of what life was like in the cotton mill culture of my youth. What follows are memories of that culture as it existed in the thirties and forties in the villages of the Bladenboro Cotton Mills.

In preparing this volume, I have restricted my observations about mill life to the decades of the thirties and forties because these were the years that I was either directly part of that life or closely associated with the men and women who worked in the Bladenboro Cotton Mills and were economically dependent on the company for their livelihood. For me, the people and events of those years have always been easy to recall—almost as if it were yesterday. These years, of course, were my growing-up years, years when people and events registered with sufficient impact not only to remember later but to play an essential role in determining who I was to become and what my perspectives on life would be. Although by the end of the forties I had begun a separation—at least a physical separation—from the culture of the mills when unexpected opportunities arose to make departure possible, my psychological roots in the mill culture of that era remain as strong as ever, never allowing for a total escape.

In deciding what subjects to include in this book to give an authentic picture of the world that my father had concluded was "gone," I was guided by strong, vivid personal memories that were validated by past conversations with my parents, aunts, uncles, and others (most of whom are now deceased) about life as it was in the villages and workplaces of the Bladenboro Cotton Mills in southeastern North Carolina. I was also guided by professional perspectives derived from years of teaching and writing about labor history. Consequently, the following chapters are not the result of intensive, historical research into the general cotton mill culture. They are not rooted in the work of other scholars who have specialized in that culture. (For readers interested in that culture, I have included a short suggested reading list.) Instead, using memory and reflection, I have topically reconstructed life as lived and perceived in and around the Bladenboro Cotton Mills during the Depression and war years of the thirties and forties. This was the world that my father shared with hundreds of other men and women workers during my youth. This was the world that, like the Old Mill village, is now "gone" forever, except in the hearts and memories of a very few survivors.

As the following chapters reveal, the vanished world of my father was complex and diverse, filled with men and women who did the best they could do under prevailing circumstances. Fresh from surrounding farms and with few opportunities, they were neither sophisticated nor educated people in a formal sense, a fact often used by other sections of the community as cause to disparage and "look down" on them with disdain. Like their counterparts in scores of cotton mills throughout the South, unfortunately, not much was expected of them by people outside the villages except, of course, to run the machines of the mills. Even so, most of the men and women of the Bladenboro Cotton Mills were durable and courageous people who made the most of what life offered their generation. Although not flawless, most were hardworking and responsible individuals who took their work, families, religion, and obligations seriously. Such people filled the world that my father bemoaned as "gone."

Today, if one approaches Bladenboro from the west along Highway 211, in the distance one sees a towering smokestack that once dominated the mill villages and the surrounding countryside. The smokestack and the mills, which are no longer in production, remain the last vestiges of a way of life that has become nearly extinct. But even these visual reminders are endangered and will soon disappear. In April and May of 2001, workers dismantled the 1923 New Mill. Its sturdy beams of heart lumber from former stands of longleaf yellow pine, its marked flooring that for years withstood the heavy weight of textile machinery and the pounding footsteps of thousands of workers, its hundreds of thousands of unusual bricks—all were destined for reuse, perhaps in faraway places. For a while, at least, the Old Mill remains, serving as a warehouse facility. When in time it, too, is dismantled—as it surely will be—the last physical evidence of a thriving working-class community of villages and mills that constituted my father's world will be truly "gone." For several generations of workers who walked the aisles and tended the machines of the Bladenboro Cotton Mills, nothing will remain to mark and honor their lives and labor.

Chapter 1

Maggie's Gold

Like many southern companies during the years of the Great Depression, the Bladenboro Cotton Mills issued specie money for use in its company store in order to recapture a portion of the wages paid to its workers. It took the form of coins in denominations of the dollar and fifty-, twenty-five-, ten-, and five-cent pieces. The coins were made of an alloy of some kind, golden in color, and were similar in size to U.S. coins.

The usual procedure for their issue was for a mill worker to draw the coins against his "time," that is, the hours of unpaid labor he had accumulated in the mills. However, if he had incurred debts at the company store, as was so often the case, he might draw the coins against his future earnings, thus adding to his debt. The pay period in the Bladenboro mills until the forties was bimonthly. At the end of every two weeks, Henry ("Hen") Freeman, the mill's paymaster for years, handed out the pay envelopes at the end of the shifts at some central point in each of the two mills that was easily accessible to departing workers. At these bimonthly paydays, a worker who had drawn company specie often found that he had little money in his pay envelope. A checklist informed him how much of his wages had been deducted and credited to his store account, rent, the doctor, and insurance.

The company store was located at the east end of "mill no. 1" (the one built first, in 1912, commonly called the Old Mill) adjacent to the Old Mill village. At the rear of the store to the left of the meat market and near the rear exit was an office with a caged window. During the thirties and early forties, two members of the mill-owning Bridger family managed this small office, issuing the company coins and transacting other business. Until his death in an automobile accident, Miller Bridger was one of these persons, a man whose response to a request for the coins, a form of credit, varied with the individual mill hand, the size of his debt, the extent of his needs, and his specific reasons for the request. According to my father, some workers judged "Mr. Miller" to be a saint, a man who was always there when their families needed food, clothing, and other items obtainable at the company store. Others saw him as the devil personified because their requests were not always immediately granted or the amount they asked for was reduced to a lesser amount.

Mrs. Margaret Bridger was the other person who worked in the office. She was a pleasant, lovely woman whose work both in the office and behind the store counters earned her the affection of many of the mill people, who called her "Mrs. Maggie." Because it was she who more often than not dispersed the golden coins after Miller had made the decision of "yes" or "no" and the amount of specie to be granted, specie became indelibly identified with her. Mill hands commonly called it "Maggie's gold," a name that stuck until the company stopped issuing the coins in the late forties.

Company money like Maggie's gold was never greatly appreciated by workers living in company towns. The only place it could be legitimately spent was in the company store, and workers everywhere sensed that the cost of every item they purchased there was higher than in other stores where they paid hard cash. Their perception of higher prices was more often than not justified; the elevated prices in company stores made it possible for mill owners to recapture a portion of the wages they had paid workers as profits on goods sold in their stores. Starkly put, the stores subtly reduced the wages of workers, who often had no alternatives but to trade in these stores. Like their counterparts in other mills throughout the South, many mill hands at the Bladenboro Cotton Mills resented Maggie's gold because they instinctively sensed that its use short-changed them in wages. Nevertheless, the use of the coins made it possible for many of them to feed and clothe their families, albeit sometimes inadequately.

Besides, there were imaginative—although expensive—ways of converting Maggie's gold into real, honest-to-goodness cur-

Mrs. Margaret ("Maggie") Bridger, whose role in issuing the golden coins of the Bladenboro Cotton Mills at the company store caused workers to name them "Maggie's gold" (c. 1945). Courtesy of Bladenboro Historical Museum.

rency of the United States. It was not uncommon for mill hands to request coins—say, five dollars' worth—against their time and then purchase cartons of cigarettes or other items at the company store for resale to small local merchants at a greatly discounted price, usually a price lower than that which the merchant would have to pay wholesale. A carton of cigarettes purchased with Maggie's gold at $1.20, for example, could be sold to someone like Bill Cain, who operated a filling station and hamburger stand on Highway 211 between the company store and town, for 80¢ cash. In this fashion, Cain and other small merchants increased their business while collecting the golden coins at a very favorable exchange rate. They later purchased items that they or their families needed from the larger and more diverse stock of the company store, coming out slightly ahead in spite of the higher prices there. In return, the mill hand got much-needed cash to use in town, accepting the loss (tantamount to a significant reduction in wages) with as good grace as possible. Converting Maggie's gold to hard cash in this manner was obviously not profitable for the worker, but in the Depression years of the thirties it was one way to work around a very restrictive system.

When local businessmen accepted Maggie's gold for their products or services it was always at the expense of the mill worker. One such businessman was W. G. Fussell, who accepted it for admission to his Lyric Theater. In the thirties and forties, movies were one of the very few forms of polished entertainment available in Bladenboro, so nearly everyone attended the Lyric unless prevented from doing so by religious conviction or other compelling reasons. A mill hand or his child could use company coins to purchase admission to the movie, but he paid a premium if he did so. For example, the price of an adult admission might be 25¢ in cash—but if Maggie's gold were used, the price was 30¢. A child's admission might be 10¢ in cash and 15¢ in company coins. This markup in the price of admission when using "mill money" was generally—though not always—accepted without complaint. Its similar incorporation into the rest of the local economy always resulted in a loss to the workers.

Generally, in transactions among themselves, mill hands accepted Maggie's gold at face value. It was not uncommon for company coins to show up in the collection plates on Sunday morning in churches attended by workers, the workers giving what they had to give. And the coins were used for gambling. Maggie's gold was thrown into the game pot along with cash with no objections. Local farmers often accepted the script for their produce—many of them, like the mill workers, were glad to have money of any kind in exchange for their milk and eggs. Furthermore, some black women and men who performed various services for the mill people (for example, "doing the wash") gladly took Maggie's gold in payment for their services. Sofa Hester, who washed clothes for our family and other mill families, accepted the coins for her work. Black domestics, who were often used when there was illness in a family, also took the Maggie's gold without complaint.

Other recipients of the coins suffered the same penalty that mill hands experienced. Although the money circulated beyond the labor force of the mill and the company store, it did so with an accepted understanding that it had less value than U.S. currency. For example, it was known that it was not convertible at face value or redeemable in U.S. currency at the store office. It could be spent at face value only at the company store or in the informal transactions just described.

Within the local economy of Bladenboro, therefore, two types of money circulated—regular U.S. currency and Maggie's gold. The latter was second-rate money, placed into circulation because of the needs of specific workers who were forced to draw, for whatever reason, advances on their wages between the bimonthly paydays. The system obviously served the interests of the mill owners or it would not have been instituted. (About two miles west of Bladenboro was a small lumber town called Butters, where the Butters Lumber Company issued similar kind of coins for the same reasons.) Nonetheless, the system definitely relieved a difficult cash flow problem during the Great Depression. Despite the penalty for its use, Maggie's gold was handy for the workers, for it permitted them to reach out beyond the company store and tap into the regular local economy, allowing them to acquire and enjoy products and services they otherwise would not have been able to obtain. Mrs. Maggie's golden coins helped to ease somewhat the harshness of the Depression—but at the cost of some workers' resentment.

My father never developed the resentment or hostility toward the Bridger family, or mill owners, that was often a product of this coinage system. He expressed a high regard for "Mr. Miller," taking pride in the fact that he "could go to Miller Bridger and get whatever I wanted" while some of his fellow workers couldn't get a "dime." But even as a small child I knew that my father had a reputation as a "hard worker," an "honest man" who was as "good as his word," one who paid his debts even if it took forever. As a small boy living in the Old Mill village, I was sent to the company store with instructions to draw Maggie's gold and purchase this item or that. Not until I was much older did I discover that my father had told both Mrs. Maggie and Mr. Miller that when I went to the store and asked for anything, they should let me have it. He would "stand for it." They honored his instructions, knowing that he stood behind their issuance of the coins to me. This arrangement reflected a complicated pattern of trust, encompassing the reliance a father placed in his son and the mutual respect and confidence between employer and employee.

As a youngster, I developed a strong liking for Mrs. Maggie, who always treated me as if I were someone special. Our friendship endured over the years. Shortly before her death in the sixties, she became bedridden with old age and infirmities. Hearing of her condition while visiting in Bladenboro, I went to see her. We reminisced about the past, especially about life in the mills and workers we both had known. Although obviously very ill, she was as gracious as ever, which made me feel fortunate to have known her. After that visit, I never saw her again. Later Mrs. Maggie quietly died in her sleep. With her death, there ended not only a bit of mill culture but an individual who had touched the lives of many workers in a positive way.

Chapter 2

FIRES IN THE NIGHT

DURING THE LATE thirties and early forties, Bladenboro Cotton Mills paid its workers after every two weeks of work, with payday being at the end of the Friday shifts. Henry ("Hen") Freeman, a short, dried-up man who served as timekeeper and paymaster for many years, computed the workers' wages from the time sheets turned into the main office by each of the mill superintendents. After making and noting the appropriate deductions for house rent, the company store, insurance, and Dr. Dewey H. Bridger, the company doctor, he placed a worker's remaining wages in a small brown envelope for distribution. The wages were in U.S. currency, not Maggie's gold. On paydays Freeman placed scores of these envelopes in a tray-like box and took them to a central place in the mills when shifts changed and handed them out to the mill hands. Before leaving the workplace, the recipients usually made a quick check of the outside notations to determine whether their "time" and deductions had been accurately calculated.

If there was a formula for computing the deductions, the workers were never able to determine what it was and how it worked. Occasionally, Freeman deducted too much for the store or too much for the doctor, making it necessary for the mill hand to insist on a return of a portion of the deductions. Or sometimes one's time was not correctly calculated, necessitating an inconvenient visit to Freeman's office for a correction. There were times, for example, when my father found it necessary to recover some of his wages from the store or the doctor in order to have *any* income from his work. His experience, I believe, was not unusual among the mill hands during this era.

Because of the long hours, the low wages, and the hard times, one might expect that all cotton mill workers of the era would cling to their wages, holding on to every possible cent and spending their hard-earned money very prudently and wisely. The majority of them did exactly that. However, some displayed an enormous facility for quickly ridding themselves of their skimpy wages on payday, a kind of reckless carelessness that ignored how difficult money was to acquire and disregarded demanding family responsibilities. Perhaps it was precisely the fact that times were hard that provoked some into such an unwise and frivolous use of their paltry pay.

In the fall of 1939, our family moved into a partially built frame house next to White Oak Original Free Will Baptist Church on Highway 211 about a quarter-mile east of the mills. It wasn't much of a house as houses go today, for it had no indoor plumbing and was unpainted and unfinished on the inside and outside. However, the move placed us next door to my parents' church and, for the purpose of this story, on the fringe of the Bryant Swamp. (Some said *in* the swamp.) From this vantage point, we had an unobstructed view into the wooded area behind the church and the house. And on payday weekends, our location offered an opportunity to observe how the members of an ever-changing band of mill workers entertained themselves with their hard-earned wages.

Standing on the back steps on Friday and Saturday nights of payday weekends, we often observed that fires had apparently been set in the woods. But strangely, however, these never spread into general wood fires like those that inevitably broke out in the spring of the year. And frequently, in the stillness of the night, voices were heard coming from the direction of the red glow among the trees and brush. It took a while to solve this mystery, much longer than it should have, because as a boy I knew every path through those woods, which stretched from the cotton mills across the Seaboard Railroad to the Bridger fields near Uncle Jim Hester's house and eastward to Bladenboro, or "the Boro" as some of the old-timers called it. Furthermore, I had often seen the sites of the fires and observed soft drink and whiskey bottles, fruit jars, broken and crushed vegetation, and the like—evidence that gatherings of some kind had occurred there.

The explanation turned out to be quite simple. A number of the mill hands liked to gamble and drink whiskey. There was a regular group consisting of Troy Cox, Fred Williams, Leslie Thompson, Jack Cain, and others that regularly retired to the woods shortly after being paid. There they would be joined in their reveling by a steady stream of fellow workers who seemed anxious to be plucked of their wages.

Taking a shortcut through the woods one Saturday morning while on my way to Pine Ridge west of town to deliver the *Grit*, I stumbled upon a group of six or eight men sitting or squatting on the ground around a brown army blanket covered with cards and money—greenbacks, coins, and Maggie's gold. It was obvious that the poker game and heavy drinking had been long under way. A number of empty whiskey bottles and fruit jars were scattered about, and several of the men were very intoxicated or "high as a kite"—so much so that they were in no condition to play poker or do anything else. They could barely sit upright and hold the cards. Nearby were the dying embers of the fire that had provided light and warmth during the night. For the first time, I had an answer to the red glow in the woods that never seemed to spread.

Absorbed in the game, the men ignored my presence. Much to my surprise, I discovered that a favorite relative, a man who ran a set of spinning frames near my father in the last-built mill, "no. 3" (commonly called the New mill), was involved in this game. Like the rest, he, too, ignored my presence. I leaned against a tree and watched the men as they shuffled and dealt the cards, cursing their luck and each other when fortune slipped away into the brush.

Arguments erupted over who had the winning hand and over alleged cheating. Violence hovered at the edge of the circle. Exhausted from work and lack of sleep, boozed up, and risking desperately needed wages on the flip of a card, they glared and scowled at each other. I could sense the tension that filled the air. The game nearly broke up when one player, losing a hand, lunged at the winner, scattering money, cards, and bottles in all directions. The two were soon separated. The fight was over as quickly as it had begun, and the game resumed as if nothing had happened, accompanied as before by loud and boisterous cursing.

The stakes were high, although not in terms of the amount of money involved, for few of these men then had a take-home pay of more than twenty or thirty dollars, if that much. The stakes were high because, except for credit at the company store, some of the players were risking their meager net earnings of the past two weeks in a desperate gamble for more—more, perhaps, for the wives and families who had not seen them since they had left for work on Friday. However, their intoxication enhanced the likelihood that their hopes for some easy money would not be realized.

This poker game was not the last that I witnessed in the woods. As a newsboy who sold the *Grit*, I had customers—a very few, I might add—who lived near the New Mill village and Pine Ridge on the extreme west end of town or in the Negro section on the extreme east end. In order to reduce the distance that I had to walk, I often took a shortcut through the woods and frequently found a poker game in progress. I was astounded to discover that some of the mill hands spent most of the weekend there gambling and drinking even when the weather was very cold.

From time to time, they asked me to go for food and drink, usually a sack of hamburgers and hotdogs and soft drinks from Bill and Mollie Cain's filling station/grill located not far away, for which I received from the men more money than I earned selling the *Grit*. The Cains sold their hotdogs and hamburgers very cheaply—six for a quarter. The men were thus able to eat without interrupting their game, leaving it only to heed nature's call in the woods.

I came to realize that a few of the "regulars" in these games were low-level supervisors who, while fond of the bottle themselves, always seemed to be the least intoxicated in the games. The supervisors were conspicuous because, unlike ordinary mill hands who nearly always wore bibbed overalls, supervisors, even minor ones like section hands and so on, usually wore belted khaki pants. On more than one occasion, it occurred to me that these people were using the games to pick up extra "wages" from men too drunk to realize that they were being swindled.

Although stories frequently circulated of fights, knifings, and drunken brawls stemming from these marathon games, they continued. For among some of the mill workers the gambling instinct, combined with great recklessness, was very strong.

I also observed this gambling proclivity when visiting the local pool hall, recognized by all the respectable citizens of the town as a den of iniquity, a place decent people did not frequent. Nevertheless, there were very few young men growing up in Bladenboro who did not visit Pelo Lockamy's pool hall (the ownership of which constantly changed) and shoot pool on one of his tables. It was a place where a number of the younger mill hands gathered on Friday afternoons and Saturdays for social and other purposes, one of which was to gamble.

The pool hall, situated close to Azzie Hardin's barbershop (itself a kind of local working-class institution for many years), was a long, rectangular room with two large plate glass windows fronting the street. Its door opened directly onto the street and, during the spring, summer, and fall, it usually remained wide open so that anyone passing by could see what went on inside. Through that door passed some of the most talented billiard players—or "sharks," as we called them—that one can imagine. I am sure that some of these fellows "earned" as much shooting pool on the weekends as they did in the mills. From late Friday afternoon until closing time on Saturday night, the best of them played "odd-ball" for a nickel a ball, stopping only to eat and respond to the calls of nature.

Among the best players were Allen Cox, Elmer Guyton, and Earl Hughes—all mill hands—and there were others whose names I can't recall. Probably the best of the lot was Guyton, a tall, lean fellow who could do remarkable things with a cue stick and a billiard ball. As a youth he had been injured in a gun accident that left him badly scarred on the left side of his face. His vision, coordination, and nerves, however, had definitely not been affected. Playing pool with Guyton for money was asking to be taken to the cleaners. Yet weekend after weekend the suckers lined up to be fleeced, five or ten losing two, three, and four dollars before quitting. Watching these sure losers play Guyton was like watching the drunks—also sure losers—play poker in the woods. The question—why did they do such a stupid thing?—always arose when I watched them. Why risk hard-earned money when losing was virtually assured? But play they did, losing several dollars each outing.

Most of the mill hands I knew while growing up in Bladenboro were not gamblers. On the contrary, they were honest and responsible people, earning their money the hard way in hard times and not inclined to risk it frivolously in games of chance. However, there were some workers who seemed strongly motivated to risk their meager wages in the most uncomfortable of environments.

Chapter 3

THE DOCTORS AND
THE MILL HANDS

FROM THE TWENTIES through much of the forties, two doctors principally provided medical services for textile workers and other residents of Bladenboro. Dr. Sankey S. Hutchinson began his practice before the 1920s, and Dr. Dewey H. Bridger, a member of the mill-owning family, followed in 1922 after completing his training at Jefferson Medical College in Philadelphia. Thus the town of Bladenboro was fortunate to have two practicing physicians. Hutchinson was, of course, older than Bridger, a fact that imposed certain limitations and constraints on his practice. He was not, for example, as willing to make house calls in the middle of the night as was the younger Bridger. And because he was not in any way associated with the Bladenboro Cotton Mills, he was less tolerant than Bridger about the nonpayment of fees for his medical services. As the Depression of the thirties spread, these factors nudged the workers toward the younger Bridger; Hutchinson had fewer patients among them.

My first encounter with Hutchinson, who was a tall, bald, and angular man, occurred on the eve of my third birthday. In 1932, when our family lived in the Old Mill village, my mother became very ill and needed someone to care for her during the day while my father worked in the mill. As my father and I rode with Joe Stubbs, a section hand in the Old Mill, to obtain the service of Beth Purdy, a black woman, Stubbs, who was nearly blind, ran his old Chevrolet off Highway 211 during a driving rainstorm, struck a culvert, and plunged into a deep hole of water just east of White Oak Original Free Will Baptist Church. When the front of the car filled with water, we nearly drowned. At great risk to himself, my father saved me by holding me above the water. Unfortunately, a sliver of glass cut a gash dangerously close to my right eye. When the wreck was discovered, some passersby lifted me out of the car through the rear window and rushed me to Dr. Hutchinson, who treated the wound. Fortunately, the cut had not involved the eye.

Nearly ten years later, when I was struck by a bicycle while taking supper to my father (who now worked in the New Mill), I was again taken to Hutchinson for emergency treatment of deep cuts, this time on my upper lip and left arm. And several years later, following a very serious cut on the ankle from stepping on a broken fruit jar in a sugarcane patch, I was again taken to Hutchinson, who clamped the wound.

It was Hutchinson who was available to treat these emergencies, although Bridger had become our family physician shortly after his arrival in Bladenboro. My father had "changed" doctors following a dispute with Hutchinson over access to medical records that doctors had compiled about my mother while she was a patient at Duke University Hospital in Durham. But whether the patient was his or not, Hutchinson was always available if needed to treat the families of mill workers.

I liked Dr. Hutchinson. As a young man, I was always in and out of his drugstore, which was located near the southeast corner of the town's major intersection where east-west Highway 211 and north-south Highway 242 crossed. He was frequently there when I entered his store, always munching on a bit of chewing tobacco and ready to talk with anyone. His drugstore was most unusual for the time. It had the usual run of drugstore merchandise, of course—including a soda fountain, sundries, a few chairs and tables, and so on. And in the rear, partitioned off from the rest, was a suite of rooms where Hutchinson examined his patients, and compounded and dispensed the medicines that he prescribed. But the store was more than a drugstore. For years signs up and down Highway 211 advertised "Get It At Hutchinson's." "It" was a host of items not then usually found in local drugstores: cameras, watches, rings, and bus tickets. My friend Sydney Edwards once theorized that "It" meant anything from sex to horse collars; however, I don't think that Sydney ever tested his theory by asking. Hutchinson, Theron Pait, and later a Miss Doshe Butler (an elderly lady who, unfortunately, impressed me as being very unattractive) presided over this emporium of diverse products.

In addition to practicing medicine, dispensing drugs, and looking after his drugstore (which during the forties also housed the local Trailways bus station, operated by Mrs. Dora Butler), Hutchinson had other business interests. He owned a chain of drugstores, located in several small towns in the area, and a dairy farm. Directly across Front Street from his drugstore in Bladenboro, Hutchinson also owned a brick, L-shaped building that wrapped around the southwest corner of the 211–242 intersection. At one time it housed on its second floor the town's only hotel, which catered to traveling salesmen. The hotel business was a singular failure in the thirties and forties because of lack of demand. With the exception of W. G. Fussell's Lyric Theater, other businesses located in the building at street level—diners, groceries, restaurants—also had short lives.

Nevertheless, Hutchinson was a forward-looking and innovative man. Once, during the forties, he planted castor bean plants on a large vacant lot near his home on Front Street. Rumors circulated that he was producing his own castor oil, a highly effective purgative then given to children in large doses, usually in the spring, to produce a "cleaning out." That project apparently failed. Although the plants flourished, Hutchinson never grew them again. During the forties, he also planted acres of grapevine seedlings in the Sandhills south of town off the Evergreen road. Rumors spread that he planned to enter the wine-making business. This enterprise also collapsed, probably because no one in the area knew much about tending grape arbors. His age, his business interests, and his service in civil organizations such as the Bladen County Board of Education gradually pushed his declining medical practice into the background.

In time, the mill people came to rely almost exclusively on Bridger, although farmers and blacks continued to use Hutchinson's services—especially in emergencies. I recall a very hot Sunday afternoon when someone drove a flat-bottom truck into town and parked it in front of his drugstore. Lying on his stomach in the

truck bed was a writhing, bare-backed black man whom someone had shot in the back with a load of bird shot. Hutchinson
was called. Surrounded by a group of wide-eyed, gawking youngsters like myself, he proceeded calmly and methodically to re-
move the bird shot and douse the man's peppered back with an
antiseptic while his patient moaned and groaned in agony. On
that summer afternoon, Hutchinson's bald head, which always
looked as if it had just been waxed and polished, was covered
in sweat like his patient's back. After treatment, the man was
taken away as he had come—that is, in the back of the truck.
During the forties, Hutchinson more and more became the town's
back-up doctor to whom people turned when Bridger was unavail-
able. However, Hutchinson had loyal patients who would see no
one else.

Hutchinson was a fine man, although many people thought
badly of him when he occasionally refused to make a house call
in the middle of the night because of his age. A Presbyterian
who was a pillar of his church, he impressed me because of his
friendship and his readiness to stop and talk. While he served
on the Bladen County Board of Education, the state added a
twelfth grade, which really interposed a new eighth grade and
did little to change the upper high school curriculum. When he
discovered that I was teaching at Williams Township School in
Columbus County, he called me aside one day and asked my
opinion about the new curriculum. I was nineteen at the time.
His request naturally pleased me, even more so when he listened
attentively to what I had to say.

Some time later, I learned that he had discussed with others
the possibility of his financially helping me to attend medical
school with the understanding that I would return to practice in
Bladenboro. However, he *never* discussed this possibility with me.
He may have seen in me some potential for medicine from a brief
episode that occurred in 1944 when my grandfather William Asie
Suggs died. Hutchinson had been called to confirm the death. As
he came into the death room he found me giving first aid to Aunt
Clara Tyler, a spinner in the Old Mill, who had fainted.

After I left Bladenboro for military service, I saw him only infrequently before his death. Unlike Bridger, Hutchinson's influence on the medical well-being of the mill workers and their families declined rapidly in the forties. Nevertheless, he was an individual who had done much for all the citizens of Bladenboro, including the people who lived in the mill villages west of town.

Because Bridger was a member of the mill-owning family, his practice became inextricably woven into the lives of the workers. A story circulated that as a boy he had become interested in medicine when the town's old doctor, seeing him standing idle on a street corner one day, had stopped his buggy and asked Bridger to drive him out into the country to see a patient. From that time on, according to the story, Bridger drove the buggy and accompanied the aging doctor as he made house calls. With other brothers and cousins managing the mills, directing mercantile interests, and controlling the town's only bank and other businesses, Bridger may have sought in medicine a different channel for his talents.

With so many workers and their families, he had an assured patient constituency. From 1922 until his death in the late 1960s from bone cancer, he was the physician in town who usually cared for the immediate medical needs of the mill hands and their families. From time to time younger doctors (including a nephew, Clarence Bridger) set up more modern medical practices in Bladenboro, but they always left for one reason or another. Consequently, until Bridger's energies began to wane with age and illness, he remained the doctor most frequently called to treat the mill hands.

I have no recollection of my first contact with Bridger, which occurred when the family lived in the Old Mill village. During the twenties and thirties, Bladenboro women usually had their babies at home, the doctor or a midwife coming to assist in the delivery. My mother had experienced medical problems in the early stages of her pregnancy, so Bridger had been consulted. Consequently, my father expected that he would make the delivery when the time arrived. As that time drew near, however, Bridger left town to visit the state fair in Raleigh. As fate would have it, he was

Dr. Dewey H. Bridger, a dedicated and caring physician, whose presence in the mill villages of the Bladenboro Cotton Mills during the thirties and forties was frequent and conspicuous (c. 1950). Courtesy of Dewey H. Bridger, Jr.

away when my mother went into labor, so Aunt Mary Edwards, a midwife who often assisted him with deliveries, was hurriedly called. She came to our house down near the bay in the Old Mill village and made the delivery, giving me, my mother later said, my "first spanking." On the following day, Bridger dropped by to see that all was well. My father was reluctant to pay him for the delivery because he had not actually performed the service, but he eventually did.

My first personal recollections of Bridger start at an early age. En route to a house call in the Old Mill village, he naturally attracted much attention from curious boys like me. Unlike the old doctor who drove a buggy, Bridger rode in a long Buick chauffeured by a black man named Creighton Lacy. The mere presence of a car in the village was enough to draw everyone's attention, but a big car driven by a black man who sat passively in the car while the doctor made the house call was certain to create a stir. In the early thirties, Bridger's car moving slowly along the sandy and deeply rutted village streets was a common sight. And when it was seen parked in front of a worker's house with Lacy waiting patiently at the wheel, everyone knew that there was sickness in that household. Any illness rapidly became public knowledge in the tightly knit community of the village.

Because my mother had a badly damaged heart valve caused by rheumatic fever, Bridger frequently came to our house. Over the years, I was able to observe him perhaps much more than other children in the village. My contacts with him were so frequent that it is difficult to single out any particular one, so I am left with a collage of impressions. Later, as a teenage boy in the early forties when my father worked at the shipyards in Wilmington during World War II, it was not unusual for me to walk the half mile from our home (now out of the village beside White Oak Original Free Will Baptist Church) in the middle of the night to "fetch" the doctor. Bridger never failed to come, regardless of the hour. Toward us and toward mill families who needed his services, he was generous with his time and his skills. Furthermore, his patients had great confidence in his ability. My mother thought very highly of him, so much so that his presence during a moment of crisis with her heart seemed to ease her anxiety and lift her spirits.

Among sick mill people he was much in demand, not only because he was a Bridger but because of his patience, his calm reassuring demeanor, and his ready accessibility.

Certain images of Bridger at work are therefore permanently fixed in my mind. One of the most enduring, of course, is that of him sitting beside my mother's sickbed, stethoscope in hand, listening to her heart. It is a scene that I am not likely to forget because I was so terribly frightened at the prospect of her death.

Another image of Bridger endures that I would like to forget. Fred Davis, another close friend, was struck and killed by a car on Highway 211 in front of the home of Leland and Rachel Shipman, both workers in the mills. Hearing the thud of impact and thinking that my younger brother, Charles, had been struck, I rushed to the scene and found the crumpled body before a crowd quickly gathered in the dusk. A blanket was brought from the Shipmans' house and placed over the body. Bridger was called. And while flashlights and headlights burned brightly in the dark, Bridger examined the body. He then turned to Roy Davis, who was a section hand in the Old Mill, and softly told him that his son was dead. The scene cannot be erased from memory.

Another image is that of Bridger's small waiting room located, as was Hutchinson's, at the back of his drugstore. It seemed always full as he met his patients on a first-come, first-served basis. Blacks and whites commingled there when every other place was segregated. Consultations and treatment were not very private because there was no air conditioning other than hand fans, and the doors and windows remained open. But that crowded small waiting room, with Bridger's diplomas from Wake Forest College and Jefferson Medical College hanging on the wall, with drugstore customers stopping to talk to patients sitting on hard wooden benches before leaving through a side office entrance, and with the sound of Bridger and his patients discussing their problems—is the backdrop for a strong image of a dedicated, overworked small-town doctor.

With the Great Depression raging in the thirties and with workers often on short-time (reduced shifts) or out of work, low-paid mill workers found it difficult to pay their medical bills and other debts. Nevertheless, as part of the mill-owning family, Bridger was somewhat insulated from the inability of his patients to pay for his services. At least this was true for the mill workers. He had an arrangement with the mill management whereby payments of fees were deducted from the wages of mill hands who owed him. Sometimes it happened that his deductions left the worker with little in his pay envelope, especially if he had other deductions for rent of a company house and debts at the company store. Mill hands who thus found themselves without income could accept their situation in silence or complain.

Excessive deductions or errors in calculating wages always brought immediate complaints from my father. On several occasions he requested that Bridger return a portion of his deducted wages. Over the years, however, his medical bills accumulated. When he left the cotton mills to work in the Wilmington shipyards during the war, his first financial goal was to repay Bridger in full. He did.

But unless workers went in and inquired about such things, they had no idea what they owed Bridger. As I recall, no statements were ever sent to his patients during the thirties. (Billing was instituted later, after the war.) Many workers never inquired about what they owed and, consequently, knew nothing about the extent of their debt. But still they paid it, out of their wages. However, before his death, Bridger instructed that all outstanding debts of former patients be forgiven.

Like Hutchinson, Bridger also had substantial financial interests in Bladenboro. He owned farms that were worked by tenant farmers. One of his tenants was my Uncle Woodrow Edwards, one of my mother's two brothers. Bridger probably also owned substantial interest in the Bladenboro Cotton Mills and business property in the town, including a partial ownership in the so-called Bridger block, whose upstairs housed the offices of the Bladenboro Cotton Mills and whose downstairs consisted of the post office, a dry cleaning establishment, Elizabeth Dunn's beauty parlor, the drugstore, Charlie Bell Ward's barber shop, Tom Hale's grocery, Ed Lewis's furniture store, and the Bank of Bladenboro. Several of these businesses, including the post office, were burned out in the forties. Like Hutchinson, Bridger owned one of the finest houses on Front Street, the "Street of Beautiful Homes."

How good were the medical services provided to the mill workers by Hutchinson and Bridger? Answers to this question necessarily rest on personal experiences. With two doctors in town during the twenties through the forties, medical services probably were more than satisfactory for a small mill town. Some such communities lacked doctors entirely. Of course, there were no hospitals in Bladenboro or anywhere in Bladen County until much later. Bridger and Hutchinson made frequent referrals to Baker and Johnson Hospitals in Lumberton, located about thirteen miles west on Highway 211. If a problem was unusually serious, they referred patients to Duke Hospital in Durham or to the Bowman Gray Baptist Hospital in Winston-Salem—both hospitals associated with medical schools.

Generally, despite the obvious limitations that marked their practices (for example, they compounded their own prescriptions because there were no trained pharmacists in Bladenboro until after World War II), Bridger and Hutchinson served the people of the mill villages and the town well. There was an enormous social, financial, and educational difference between them and their patients, to be sure, especially the patients living in the two mill villages. Nevertheless, they provided a level of service without which the workers and residents of the town and surrounding countryside would have suffered greatly in an era of limited public health facilities.

Chapter 4

THE DOPE WAGON

WORKING IN A cotton mill in the thirties and early forties was a nerve-racking experience. This was certainly the case in the works of the Bladenboro Cotton Mills where, as a boy during the summer, I frequently took lunch to my father when he worked the first shift or dinner when he worked the second shift. Throughout the mills, rumbling overhead shafts turned a belt and pulley system which, when combined with the whine of thousands of whirring spindles on the machines, produced a deafening roar that bombarded the mill hand long before he entered the workplace.

To the unaccustomed ear such as mine, the din created by the machines seemed at first unbearable. But to the mill hands, the noise of the mill was part of their lives, something to which they were thoroughly accustomed. The noise, which turned every conversation among the workers into a shouting match, was so much a part of the work environment that the mill hands felt a strange uneasiness at the pervasive stillness produced when the mills were idle because of lack of orders or the observance of Sunday.

Workers whose rented houses were located in either the Old or the New Mill villages ("mill hills" was the common name for the two company-owned villages located near the mills) resided where the roar of the machines reached out to touch their lives even when off the job. When the mills ran, the noise was always present throughout the villages—a constant presence from which there was no escape. Among the workers, it produced a love-hate, bittersweet attitude toward the mills. When the mill hands lay in bed in the dead of night, they could hear the mills humming seductively, the sound providing the comforting knowledge that upon arising in the morning they had work. Yet the nearby subdued roar was also a nagging reminder that they were ensnared, probably for the rest of their lives, in a system from which neither they nor their children were likely to escape. The song of the mills thus conveyed messages of both hope and despair to the workers.

In walking the unpaved streets from their company-owned house toward the mills, workers were embraced by an increasing din until, stepping into the workplace, they entered a shift-long bedlam that jangled the nerves and made them long wistfully for the banks of the Black or South Rivers, the Big Swamp, the outdoors, the seashore, the home—any place but where they were trapped for a noisy working shift. Noise, heat, lint, demanding machines, and constant movement enveloped them on the job, causing them to seek relief however they could find it.

Some workers were fortunate to have a measure of relief in the structure of their jobs. For example, the doffers, usually young males with strong backs and deft fingers, were responsible for a number of spinning frames. Sometimes they "caught up," permitting them to go outside the mills and rest for a short while until it was time to doff again. But most workers were tied to machines that demanded constant tending. These workers had to find relief in snatched moments. My father, who worked in the New Mill running sets of spinning frames, rarely took a sustained break to eat the food that I brought to him. The yarn broke frequently; loose ends had to be tied. Consequently, he ate on the run, setting his plate and his fruit jar of iced tea on the end of a frame and grabbing the food when his work permitted. Many workers were tied to their machines in this manner—for example, my Uncle David James Pait (whom my father affectionately called "Crockett"), who tended nearby frames. The pressure to "make production," or the expected number of "hanks," the constant roar of the machines, and the ever-present hazards of running belts and pulleys made the working environment a nerve-racking experience that often led to accidents. My mother's Uncle Jim Hester had a hand and arm crippled when his clothing was caught in a moving belt.

Late one afternoon while returning home after taking my father's dinner to the New Mill, I crossed the bridge over the pond on Highway 211 that separated the Old from the New Mill and saw Fletcher ("Flutch") Thompson leaning out a window of the Old Mill and motioning for me to come over. Thompson had worked in the mills for years and looked consumptive—stooped, with round shoulders and a caved-in chest. Handing me money, he asked that I go to Bill Cain's filling station (the company store was then closed for the day), purchase a Coca-Cola and a small bottle of spirit of ammonia, and bring them to him. He said that he was "nervous" and needed something to settle him down. I did as Flutch requested. Upon my return, much to my surprise he emptied the tiny flat bottle of ammonia into the Coke and drank the mixture. I later learned that mixing Coke and ammonia for the nerves was not an uncommon practice among mill workers and others. (When I later worked at Guyton's Drug Store in Whiteville during the summer of 1945 while playing American Legion baseball, I discovered that it was not unusual for a few local businessmen en route to work in the morning to stop by the fountain for a Coke mixed with a teaspoon of spirit of ammonia to steady their nerves for the day ahead.) The conditions in the mills—the noisy machines, the lint-filled air, the extreme heat (especially in the summer), the inability of most workers to escape even temporarily—all made many mill hands not only nervous but gave them headaches, clogged nasal passages, tired feet and legs, a chronic cough, and a predisposition to seek relief with various remedies.

Sometime in the thirties, the owners had the mill carpenters construct a box on wheels that was small enough to move in the alleys between the machines. The box was about the size of a "drink box" (a box once used by storekeepers to "ice" their soft drinks) with trays on top. Each day the wagon, filled with soft drinks—Coke, Pepsi, RC, and so on—was wheeled into the mill directly to the workers on the job. On the top of the device were trays loaded with snack foods—nabs (packaged crackers with peanut butter filling), candy bars, peanuts, and the like. But a very important item, probably placed there on demand, was an ample supply of headache remedies of all kinds—aspirin and powders such as BC, Goodies, and Standback. This wagon, which was a miniature concession stand on wheels, was appropriately called the "dope wagon." This name may have been derived from the old days when Coca-Cola contained cocaine as one of its ingredients until prohibited by law. More likely, however, it stemmed from the workers' observation of their enormous consumption of headache medication. They accurately called the concession wagon the "dope wagon." That is what it was. When workers asked for a soft drink, usually Coca-Cola, they would generally say, "Let me have a dope."

Later, after World War II, the practice of sending the dope wagon through the mills ceased with the installation of new machinery. The mill owners built a very small brick store near the New Mill at the southwest end of a second wooden bridge that crossed the pond and connected the Old and New Mills and cotton houses. There, workers with a few minutes of freedom could purchase soft drinks and snacks for themselves and for others unable to get away from their machines. Not surprisingly, this new store became known among the workers as the "dope house."

The mill hands, of course, did not see the dope wagon or the dope house as sources of dangerous drugs that would harm them in any way. However, working conditions in the mills did encourage a substantial use of aspirin, headache powders, ammonia and, in many instances, excessive use of alcohol off the job. Even now I remember an unknown worker opening up a package of BC powder—a widely advertised headache remedy of the time that provided two doses for a nickel—opening his mouth wide to pour in all the white substance, and washing it down with a swig of Coke. Unfortunately, some workers found it necessary to use these remedies daily in order to make it through their shifts, to temporarily reduce or eliminate the jangled nerves and throbbing heads produced by the pressures of the mills. The dope wagon and the dope house were indispensable for some.

Chapter 5

A Woman Named Sofa

Sofa Hester was a remarkable woman. I say this even though her life touched my adult years only sporadically and my observations of her then were therefore limited. Our principal contacts occurred when I was young and very impressionable, and perhaps this is why I look back on her with so much affection and admiration. Others looking at her life might not see her as remarkable, but I am convinced that my assessment of her is correct and accurate. When I reflect on the array of colorful and rich personalities who enriched my youth, Sofa is among them and high on the list. Although she was not a mill employee, her work as a washwoman nevertheless made her a visible presence in both the Old and New Mill villages. She was part of those complex relationships that characterized life there during the thirties and forties.

Because Sofa was the family washwoman for years, it might seem strange that she should rank so high among my favorite people to remember. I am not sure that I can answer why this is so. She washed clothes for my family for so long that I can't remember when my memories of her begin. It seems that like many other people of my youth, she was someone who was always there, a kind of reliable presence. She always arrived at our home very early on Wednesday or Saturday mornings to do the wash. Rain or shine, hot or cold—unless she was sick, she was there. Sofa was totally dependable and, for our family, this attribute of character was very much appreciated because of the chronic illness of my mother. We were not, however, the only beneficiaries of her work. Sofa had a regular clientele of mill and town families for whom she washed. Her service was in much demand because she always did a good job—sometimes with much fuming and fussing, but always a good job. I would not hesitate to call her an "expert" at washing clothes.

Perhaps it was those qualities of reliability and expertise—among others—that have fastened her image so strongly in my mind.

Physically, Sofa was an impressive woman because of the sense of strength that she exuded. She was tall with broad shoulders, and it was obvious that her use of the washboard had enhanced her muscular development. I don't think I ever recall seeing a more powerfully built woman than Sofa, nor one who seemed totally immune to the elements. Her body seemed insensitive to extreme heat and cold. Her endurance was phenomenal; she never seemed to tire or "wear out." Although she had a fierce countenance, she laughed easily, exposing teeth that age and a constant use of snuff had left badly in need of repair. Even so, she was a handsome woman and black as the ace of spades. Her temper was quickly aroused if she thought herself mistreated, and her vocabulary was full of "cuss words" that she could release in a torrent. But most of all, I remember her as a determined woman who went about her business of washing clothes with hands almost white from overuse of bleach, someone who minded her own business and expected others to do the same.

When I was about ten or twelve years old, I was expected to help Sofa with the wash. At this time my parents had moved out of the Old Mill village into a house directly east of White Oak Original Free Will Baptist Church. Helping Sofa was not difficult during the summertime. My job was to gather the wood to burn around the wash pot in which the clothes were boiled, fill the pot and several washtubs with water from the overflow (artesian well) located at the edge of the church yard, and help Sofa move the washed clothes in a tub out to the clothesline. Our joint effort at the wash provided an overworked, aging black woman and a young, impressionable white boy with an opportunity to know each other and to form a friendship that endured until her death in the late fifties.

My mother's attitude toward Sofa was ambivalent. A sickly woman in the thirties and forties, she admired—perhaps even envied—the extraordinary physical strength of the woman who washed her clothes. But times were difficult, and both women were inclined to be argumentative over small things of little substance. For example, once in the early forties during the war, Sofa asked for a raise, requesting that her pay for the wash be increased from seventy-five cents to a dollar—an increase that my mother thought was entirely too much. As a result, the two women had a "falling out," causing Sofa to quit. This was a disaster for the family. We had no washing machine, not even indoor plumbing. My father commuted daily to the wartime shipyards in Wilmington. I was in school, with a job in Bill Hussey's downtown grocery store on the weekends. No one else could be found to do the wash. I finally resolved this situation by locating Sofa at work in the Old Mill village and persuading her to change her mind and return to do our wash. In return I promised to pay her the extra twenty-five cents she demanded. It was not an easy decision for Sofa because she had a lot of pride, and she felt that she had been, as she put it, "wronged." She mulled over my proposal while tonguing her Railroad Mills snuff from side to side and stirring clothes in the wash pot with a long stick. She finally reluctantly agreed—each of us promising the other that my mother was not to know about the arrangement. Exploiting our friendship, I had persuaded her to return—not, however, without a little deception. I told my mother that Sofa was returning on the old terms but that it would be best not to mention the matter again. It never was while Sofa washed for us.

I was amazed at Sofa's stamina. Bladenboro had no public transportation system and few people had cars. Consequently, most people walked or stayed at home. Like most of us, Sofa walked. When she came to wash for us, she walked from her home near Richardson, which was located nearly two miles west of Bladenboro. One morning after getting the wash under way, she noticed smoke billowing up in the distance toward Richardson. For some reason, she concluded that her house was on fire. Leaving in the middle of the wash, she hurriedly walked the miles back to her home only to discover that it was the house of a relative in flames, not hers. She then walked the distance back, completed the wash and, after having a late lunch with us, hurried off to do another wash in the Old Mill village. She then again walked the distance home. In addition to her regular work, she had walked nearly eight or ten miles.

The relationship between blacks and whites in the South during this period has often been portrayed in the worst way, as if there were no affection or respect between them. But in the case of Sofa and our family, I never saw any meanness in the relationship, not even in the dispute over pay. The years of the Great Depression and the war were rough on all working families, ours and Sofa's, and this created sympathetic bonds that often transcended race. Sofa and my mother often engaged in a great deal of harmless bantering, fussing, and sometimes quarreling over trivia. But I can't count the times that Sofa sat at our table and ate lunch with us, sharing whatever we had before going on to another wash. People who sit, eat, and drink together find it difficult to dislike each other. It was that way with us.

Of course, it is impossible to know exactly how Sofa viewed her relationship with our family and other whites for whom she washed clothes. The subject was never discussed. But Sofa was a proud woman, one who would not meekly submit to perceived slights or taunts resulting from her race. Once I observed her fierce response to an unkind racial remark made by a next-door friend, who for no reason other than meanness called Sofa a "darky." Grabbing her steaming stirring stick from the wash pot, Sofa drew it back in a threatening gesture and angrily told the friend, whose mother was of dark complexion, "Listen to me, boy! Be careful what you say. If they'd dipped your mama one more time, she'd be blacker than me. So don't you ever call me 'darky' again. You hear me, boy?" He heard, understood, and promptly left. Sofa, angry and mumbling to herself, returned to her work. As for me, my friend's thoughtless remark embarrassed me into silence. And for awhile we worked together without speaking. Such an episode undoubtedly predisposed Sofa to think harshly of some, if not all, whites with whom she had contact.

My last encounter with Sofa was in the late fifties shortly before she died. My wife and I were returning to Charlotte, where

I had a teaching position. As we approached Bud Edwards's store west of town, I saw a familiar black figure. I recognized Sofa immediately. She was much older, more stooped, and her hair was white, but even then she seemed to exude strength. I pulled over to the side of the road and walked toward her with my hand outstretched, calling her name. There was instant recognition. Not satisfied with a handshake, she pulled me into her arms for a great hug. She seemed so happy to see me again and to meet my wife. It was the last time I ever saw her, but I remember her fondly as part of my growing up in a rural textile town.

Years later in the eighties, as my father and I were walking down Front Street in Bladenboro, several black women approached. Stopping them, he asked me if I recognized any one of them. Looking into their faces, I knew instantly that one of the women had to be Sofa's daughter. I was right! The features were unmistakably Sofa's. She lived again in her offspring.

Chapter 6

MILL HANDS
AND CHRISTMAS

CHRISTMAS WAS A special time in the Old and New Mill villages during the thirties. Not even the Great Depression could completely dampen the spirit of the mill hands and their families, who looked forward to the holiday season with excited anticipation. Several weeks before Christmas, evidence of its coming appeared—a candle or a decorated tree (usually a small pine or holly) here and there in the windows of the company houses, a smattering of festive decorations strung about in the company store, and an excitement among the younger mill children, who began to dream and talk about what they expected from Santa Clause.

At the same time, there was also a new level of concern among the mill hands because of the increased expenses of the season. Times were hard; money was in short supply and extremely difficult to obtain. Christmas was therefore a Janus-like season. Celebrating the birth of Christ was a hopeful event that elevated the spirit; however, the financial demands of Christmas were a sharp reminder that there was indeed much to hope for.

I don't recall that the Bladenboro Cotton Mills ever gave its employees end-of-the-year cash bonuses at any time during the thirties and forties. But at Christmas the company regularly extended a small gesture of goodwill toward its workers when it acted to assure them of a good holiday meal and their children of some special treats to mark the day. Weeks before Christmas, mill officials ordered boxes of apples, crates of oranges, stalks of bananas, pounds of candy (usually hard striped candy and chocolate drops), and bags of nuts which, upon arrival, they stored in the mill carpentry shop run by Archie Pait. The shop was located just off the wooden back bridge connecting the Old and New Mills. Shortly before Christmas, the family of each worker received a grocery sack of these items, prepared by Archie, the lead carpenter for the mills, and his crew. And there were Christmases when a turkey or a picnic ham would be thrown in. As the sacks were distributed, the name of the family was checked off a list of employees.

This practice of assuring at least a minimal amount of extras for the mill workers at Christmas extended into the war years of the early forties. During the fall of 1942, my father left the mills for a higher-paying job, starting at forty cents an hour, in the shipyards at Wilmington. When my mother heard that the mills were dispensing the annual Christmas bonus (that year a small picnic ham), she insisted that I go and request one for the family. After all, she said, it was only right to do so because my father had worked in the mills for most of the year, and he certainly deserved the ham. Reluctantly, I did as instructed, made the case for the ham to Charles Hasbrook, a longtime mill official who operated the dye plant and who knew my father, and returned with a small ham, which was very tasty.

These gifts at Christmas, though small, helped to make the season more joyful for the mill people. Furthermore, they engendered at little cost an enormous amount of goodwill toward the mill owners, who undoubtedly knew that some of their employees would have little or nothing extra for the holidays without their help.

Christmas was celebrated in other ways in the villages. While it is impossible to determine how many mill hands were churchgoers, large numbers undoubtedly attended one of the dozen churches in and around Bladenboro. Some of the churches were working-class churches close to the mills whose membership consisted exclusively of mill hands and their families. One such was our church, White Oak Original Free Will Baptist Church. Ours and similar churches presented a Christmas program, usually on Christmas Eve. Our church's preparation for the holidays generally commenced with the forming of a program committee in late November. Children were encouraged, drafted, or dragooned into participating. Scripture readings, songs, and skits built around the Christmas story composed the program year after year. At White Oak there was also an exchange of gifts following the presentation. Several weeks before the event, members of the Sunday School classes drew names to determine who would buy and receive gifts. On the night of the program, these presents were brought into the church and placed under the Christmas tree. At the end of the service, someone dressed in a Santa suit entered the sanctuary with great fanfare and, to the delight of the children, marched up front, where he dispensed the gifts under the tree. These were never expensive—ties, handkerchiefs, socks, and so on—but to hear one's name called once, maybe several times, to receive a gift was always a great thrill.

Another ritual was associated with Christmas at White Oak. On Sunday mornings throughout the year, all persons having a birthday were invited to march to the front of the church and contribute one penny for each year of their age into a small barrel-shaped bank set on the altar. The responsibility for keeping the bank with its treasure was passed around from year to year among members of the congregation. Shortly before Christmas, a special committee opened the bank and counted the money, which rarely exceeded thirty-five or forty dollars. The amount was always announced to the congregation. It was then used to buy fruit and candy for Santa's distribution in small sacks to the children of the church on the night of the program. Through such means, church members enjoyed themselves, good cheer and fellowship abounded, and the children were made especially happy.

The mill families who attended White Oak—and there were many—found the Christmas Eve celebration sustaining. Without much expense, the season was celebrated in such a way as to ameliorate the harshness of the times and life in the mills. Similar celebrations occurred in the surrounding churches, where mill hands and their families worshiped in numbers—West Bladenboro Baptist Church, the Church of God, the Fire Baptized Holiness Church—and in some of the rural churches to which a few workers belonged—Galeed, Sandy Grove, and others.

In the early thirties after the election of Franklin D. Roosevelt as president, a preschool was started in the Old Mill village. Mill hands believed that Roosevelt's New Deal provided the money for a teacher (Miss Evelyn Thompson) as well as for the food, fruit, and cod liver oil that were dispensed there. Children from both the Old and New Mill villages were eligible to attend. The company supplied an old house where the children met.

Strongly encouraged at the start by my mother, who convinced me with a switching that it was a good idea, I attended preschool there in 1933 and 1934. Each Christmas there was a program which, for many mill children, provided the very first opportunity to perform in public. I recall that my first recitation occurred in 1934, when I had to recite a portion of the Christmas story as related in the Book of Luke. That year mothers with the time gathered to hear their offspring recite and sing carols. The children who recited or sang solos walked from the kitchen, stood framed in a doorway that served as a stage, and faced an audience of anxious but beaming faces. For the group songs, however, we all jammed into the same room with the mothers, who sat patiently in straight-backed uncomfortable chairs. I remember the faces of the audience looked blurred (caused partly by the very poor lighting from a weak bulb on a drop cord dangling from the ceiling), but I also remember particularly and clearly the face of my mother, who was obviously very pleased to have her son participate in the program. I am certain that all the other mothers from the villages reacted similarly.

Christmas in the mill village and throughout the area was extremely noisy. When I was a youngster, it was customary to shoot off fireworks during the Christmas season, not on the Fourth of July as was done in other sections of the country. Catalogs from fireworks' companies in distant places arrived in early November to allow sufficient time for the Christmas orders to be shipped railway express. Various "assortments"—All American Boy, Noisy Boy, and others—could be ordered for several dollars. As a boy, I saw these catalogs but never ordered fireworks while the family lived in the mill village.

In 1937, after the family had returned to the Old Mill village after living for a short while on Pine Ridge to the west of the New Mill, my father awoke me early on Christmas morning. Somewhere he had acquired a half-dozen silver bombs, a type of firecracker that made an awful, wonderful noise when it exploded. We crossed the sandy unpaved street and fired off one of these bombs on a neighbor's front porch, provoking a lot of yelling on the inside and providing us with much amusement. Generally, Christmas Eve was marked by the popping of firecrackers throughout the Bladenboro community, not just in the mill villages. This noise gradually subsided until daybreak, when children, arising early, found more firecrackers under the tree. Christmas morning was loud in its celebration. With the mill shut down for the holidays, the air was filled with loud explosions and popping noises. Not until later years did I discover that only in the South was Christmas celebrated in such a fashion.

Our family always had a tree at Christmas—a small pine or holly that my father had cut from the nearby Bryant Swamp or the woods that covered the area. It was decorated with old-fashioned leaded icicles and other items that my mother either had made or accumulated over the years. Furthermore, although the mill years were difficult years, we always had plenty at Christmas. Before the holiday, when she was physically able to do so, my mother would bake chocolate and coconut pies, regular and Japanese fruitcakes, and chocolate and coconut cakes, spending hours preparing delicious goodies for the people expected to drop in. These would be tucked away in the "safe" (a pie safe) with her instructions not to touch. Regardless of how financially strapped the family might be, there was always an abundance of oranges, apples, bananas, and nuts of all kinds (pecans, hazel nuts, Brazil nuts, and almonds) that appeared on Christmas morning. Chicken and ham were usually on the table for that special day. My parents wanted every Christmas to be memorable even if it meant sacrifice.

Looking back on those Christmases while my father worked in the mills, I remember them as very happy occasions. Expensive gifts were never given, nor were they expected. If one had been given, I am certain that it would not have been recognized as expensive. Christmas was a time of great joy and goodwill, when family members seemed to love each other just a little bit more, when the frustration and the problems of the times were pushed aside for the moment. Hard times didn't go away for Christmas; they always hovered around the door. But on Christmas Day we forgot them. And most mill families did the same.

Chapter 7

DEATH AND THE MILL HANDS

WHILE I WAS growing up in Bladenboro, death among the working families living in the Old and New Mill villages seemed to occur frequently, caused by accidents, irrational behavior, or disease. At a very early age I became aware of how tenuous life is, how easily this precious gift can slip away. Part of this sensitivity to death, I am sure, stemmed from the chronic illness of my mother. She seemed always to be near death during my early youth. Another obvious reason was the physical and social closeness of the mill village residents—news, especially tragic news, spread very rapidly throughout the community. Thus the death of someone was a much-talked-about event wherever people gathered—whether at the kitchen table, the end of a spinning frame, the company store, or the dope house. Even a child could not escape the visible evidence of death—for example, the black hearse of J. M. Biggs that crawled the sandy ruts of the village en route to its destination.

My first contact with death among the mill hands occurred about 1933, when I was a boy of four. Across the street from our rented house in the Old Mill village lived the Tully Singletary family. The Singletarys had two daughters—Mildred, who later married R. D. Hester (the son of my mother's Uncle George, a section hand in the Old Mill), and Vivian, who married Ferris Hester (the son of my mother's Uncle Jim, whose hand and arm had been mangled in a belt and pulley accident in the New Mill). Tully was a veteran of World War I, as were a number of mill hands, like Lon Deaver, who lived on our unnamed street, and my Uncle David J. Pait, whose family lived in rooms of our rented house. Tully, unfortunately, had been terribly shell-shocked during the war. Sometime during 1933 he became very ill and died, leaving behind his wife and daughters, who were then very young. Because the family lived near us in the village, the death of Tully provided my first direct knowledge of death. The event made a lasting impression on me.

The conditions of the time made death much more vivid and personal than it is now—death had not yet become so sanitized. It was then customary for the deceased to lie in state at home, not in the insulated, cosmetic environment of the modern funeral parlor, and it was also customary as a mark of respect that family members, relatives, or friends take turns "sitting up" with the corpse throughout the night. As a friend and neighbor, my father took his turn sitting up with Tully's body in the middle of the night. Although I was only a small boy then, I can recall standing on our front porch and looking curiously across the unpaved street at the Singletary front porch, which was filled with friends, relatives, and fellow workers coming and going, standing and talking, and chewing and smoking.

Among the people in the mill village, there was a unity, a sense of oneness, that caused them to rally behind their own when a family experienced a grievous loss. This strong sense of supportive community was partly produced by their physical and general cultural isolation from surrounding residents of the town and countryside who, because of a sense of social superiority, preferred minimal contact with the villagers. This attitude helped to increase the latter's awareness of their common interests and to accelerate their movement into closer community. Tragedy further facilitated their coming together. They rallied to support neighbors facing extraordinary or tragic circumstances. The death of a loved one was a universal experience that they all could understand. Such an event was thus shared by all because lives in the village were so intimately linked by family ties, workplace relationships, and common experiences. So as Tully lay in state at home, mill hands—men and women—were constantly coming and going, paying their respect and offering to help the widow.

The most memorable event surrounding the death occurred on the day of the burial—that is, memorable from the standpoint of a small boy. The Singletarys chose to bury Tully in the Singletary Cemetery (distant relation to Tully's family) outside Butters, which lay several miles west of Bladenboro off Highway 211. At that time Butters was a thriving little lumber camp taking timber (pine and cypress) out of the Big Swamp west of the town. It then had a large boarding house, a company store, and a large mill for processing lumber. The graveyard lay beyond the mill near the edge of the swamp and was accessible only by a very narrow road and footpath.

Few mill people had automobiles in those days, and the decision to bury Tully outside of Butters created a problem. It was then customary for friends of the deceased to follow the body to the burial site, but with no cars or other transportation, it appeared that this could not be done. Yet somehow, a low flatbed truck was obtained and anyone wanting to attend the burying could do so. Consequently, a large number of people, including my father and I, climbed on the truck bed and, hanging onto each other for dear life, we rode to Butters. We approached the cemetery on the truck as far the road would allow and then dismounted and walked the rest of the way, some along the very narrow dirt road and some along the path that lay alongside the lumber mill.

Like all burials, Tully's was a mournful event—a few words from the minister, a song ("Shall We Gather at the River" or some mournful piece), the weeping of loved ones and friends, and the conspicuous lowering of the casket into the ground. As was the custom, friends and fellow workers shoveled the first dirt onto the wooden box enclosing the casket. To this day, I remember the distinctive sound it made as it hit the covering box. It was a sound not easily forgotten by a boy of four, nor were the accompanying sounds of grief and despair. After the brief ceremony, we followed the path back to the flatbed truck and crowded on for the return trip to the Old Mill village, where life renewed itself in old, familiar patterns. As the saying goes, Tully was gone but not forgotten. (In August 1979, shortly before her death, my mother and I drove to Butters and visited the cemetery where Tully had been buried more than forty-five years earlier. Much had changed, of course—the lumber mill was gone except for its concrete foundation, and the old boarding house looked ready to collapse. There was a new paved road to the cemetery. We immediately found the headstone of Tully and reminisced about the old days. Forty-five years!)

I remember another death that profoundly affected dozens of mill workers. I spoke of it briefly in chapter 3. By 1940 our family had moved from the Old Mill village into several different houses, finally settling in 1938 for a long stay in a house my parents had built beside our church, the old wooden White Oak Original Free Will Baptist Church. Although we had left the Old Mill village, our contacts with mill people remained constant because many relatives were textile workers whose families attended White Oak.

I had a very close friend named Fred Davis. Fred was the son of Roy and Ruby Davis, who worked in the mills. Because Roy was the son of my mother's Aunt Maryann, Fred and I were related, like most of the families living near the Bladenboro Cotton Mills; multiple kinship ties—some close, some distant—were the norm. Fred and I were not only related but were good friends. In the fall of 1940 we had just begun our sixth-grade year in the Bladenboro Public Schools.

One Saturday afternoon while walking along Highway 211 with a cousin, Fred darted out in front of a speeding automobile driven by old man Oliver Perry's daughter and was instantly killed. The impact of the blow threw Fred onto the highway directly in front of his Aunt Rachel Shipman's home. When the accident occurred, my mother and I were eating supper. We heard the sickening thud, the screeching brakes, and immediately concluded that my brother, Charles, who had gone with my father to visit my Aunt Clara, had been struck. Rushing out into the dusk, I ran the fifty yards up the highway where the body lay, dreading the thought that it was my brother. Bob Hester (a brother of Rachel and Maryann and a shift boss in the Old Mill) and I reached the crumpled body about the same time. Fred lay there dying, a horrible hole knocked in his forehead.

There followed a grisly scene—a gathering crowd in the growing darkness, hushed voices, a quilt from Aunt Rachel's thrown over the body, the interminable wait for the arrival of Dr. Dewey Bridger to confirm the death, the arrival and screams of Roy and Ruby. When Bridger arrived he examined Fred's body and, turning to Roy, he gently said, "Roy, he's dead," which brought forth renewed wailing and anguished moans that pierced the growing darkness. That terrible scene haunted me for years. With the doctor's pronouncement, Fred's body was wrapped in a quilt from Rachel's home, placed in the back of someone's pickup truck, and taken to the Davis home in the Old Mill village, the father riding in the truck with his dead son. There he was placed on one of the family beds to await the arrival of the undertaker.

Later, family and friends, consisting nearly entirely of mill workers, poured into the Davis home where Fred lay in state, spilling out onto the porch and into the yard. And at the funeral at White Oak, they came by the score to pay their respects. Funerals then were often long and extended services, with a minister or ministers "preaching the funeral" before a last soul-wrenching viewing of the body by the family and the entire congregation, which slowly moved past the open coffin. How grief-stricken families withstood such psychological trauma is beyond me. But out of it all seemed to come a purging release, an awareness of our mortality and the finality of death, a grudging acceptance of its reality.

They buried Fred at Oak Grove Original Free Will Baptist Church, located six or eight miles north of town off the Dublin highway. With Roy and Ruby grieving and refusing to be comforted, the mournful graveside ritual tore gaping, emotional wounds into all who were gathered there. Once again I witnessed the shoveling of dirt on the boxed casket. The thumping, hollow sounds were the same as those at the Singletary burial. Hearing those awful sounds, punctuated by the sobbing of Roy and Ruby, the onlookers again confronted their own mortality. Such experiences developed among that generation of mill workers a resignation to the inevitability of death and led them to accept it as part of life itself. It was but another dimension of suffering that had to be borne.

Older now than I had been at Tully Singletary's death and enormously affected by the death of my friend, I was more sensitive to the rallying of the mill people behind the Davis family. It seemed that all of them shared this terrible tragedy. Roy and Ruby both worked in the mills, were well known, and were active members of White Oak Church, whose members were principally relatives and mill families. Once again, their strong support came to the forefront in those hard and difficult moments. Fred's death brought forth dramatic evidence of their sharing spirit.

Not long after Fred's death, another occurred that shed additional light on how mill workers confronted this grim, final reality. My great-grandmother Exie Hester, her husband Daniel, and most of their ten children had worked in the mills. When Daniel "pased away," Grandma Exie moved in with her daughter Rachel's family. She was a wizened, shriveled-up, somewhat irascible old lady, who usually spent her days, weather permitting, sitting on the front porch leaning on her cane, dipping snuff, and accosting persons en route to and from town with a torrent of questions. In November or December of 1940 she died.

Grandma Exie was an extraordinary person. Surrounded by her brood, most of whom lived within a mile radius of the Shipman home, she demanded attention—and she got it. Somewhat devilish herself, a trait that she passed on to most of her children and grandchildren, she was often the victim of childish pranks—all of which she took in good grace despite a waspish nature. Before her death, she informed everyone that she did not want any weeping and wailing when she went on to "Glory Land." So when she died, everyone tried to respect her wishes as much as possible.

On the night before her burial, Grandma Exie lay in state in a bedroom at Rachel's while her clan came and went in bunches throughout the night. They gathered in a bedroom/sitting room across the hall, one that had a wood heater where a roaring fire was maintained. There was no sadness among these talkative descendants, most of whom worked in the mills. Tyne, a daughter, had arrived from St. Pauls, a small nearby textile town that seemed extremely distant at the time. The few others who did not live in the village had also come. Grandma Exie's death served to bring her family together in a joyful reunion. While she lay in death across the hall, her flock of children and grandchildren celebrated life.

Nearly all of the Hester clan worked in the Bladenboro Cotton Mills. One of the sons, Blaine, dabbled occasionally in farming, but the remainder were mill workers. Bob and George were low-level supervisors who placed family members into openings as they occurred. Jim was a mill hand with an impaired arm caused by an accident involving a pulley in the Old Mill. Rachel, Maryann, and the other sisters were also mill workers. The Hester family made up much of the membership of White Oak Original Free Will Baptist Church.

Kinship ties, church ties, workplace ties—all rippled out to create a support system that sustained mill workers like the Singletarys, the Davises, and the Hesters in times of crisis such as a death in the family. Each of these deaths reflected the solidarity and sense of community prevailing among the mill people.

Chapter 8

MILL VILLAGE PEDDLING

AFTER THE OPENING of the company store at the east end of the Old Mill in 1930, the majority of the mill hands made the bulk of their purchases there. The store was a separate building located on the edge of the Old Mill village and faced State Highway 211 and the tracks of the Seaboard Railroad that ran parallel to it. The store was first managed by Emmett Guyton, a veteran of World War I who had become a seasoned clerk in the Bridger Corporation store in downtown Bladenboro. In addition to selling groceries and dry goods under Guyton's direction, the store also dispensed credit to mill workers in the form of mill coinage— Maggie's gold. The company store and its credit system became inextricably part of mill life because so many workers came to rely on it for necessities.

Nevertheless, in the early thirties there was still room for the small entrepreneur who worked the Old and New Mill villages with products that the store did not stock and sometimes with products that were in direct competition with the store. However, I never knew the company to oppose these sales. As a small boy, these peddlers made an early impression on me as they moved about the village selling their wares.

One of the busiest sites in the mill complex, especially at the changing of shifts, was the area both behind and between the store and the end of the Old Mill. On any given day, there might be a steam engine shifting coal hoppers and boxcars on the rail siding running directly behind the store and along the north side of the Old Mill. Or the tractor-trailers of Grover Pait or Cary Dowless, local men who owned small trucking companies, might be parked near the dock of the Old Mill nearest the store, while mill hands trucked out and loaded boxes of neatly packaged yarn, each bound with black shiny steel tape and each stenciled with its contents and destination on the side. In addition, the human traffic here was often intense, with much coming and going from the company store as workers made last-minute purchases like a fountain "dope" before entering the mill. It was here that I have my first recollection of a peddler in the mill village. He was Alfred ("Alfie") Davis, a man I continued to know throughout my teenage years.

As a young boy of three or four, I thought Davis was ancient because of his full white beard that extended down to his chest. He lived about three miles north of Bladenboro on the Dublin road, where he owned a small acreage. He frequently loaded farm produce on a wagon, hitched up his mule, and drove to the Old and New Mill villages to sell his goods directly to the workers. Company officials permitted these sales, although occasionally some of his goods were in direct competition with the company store.

My first memory of Davis is of him standing at the end of his wagon dispensing milk from a large container into fruit jars brought by women customers. Parked in the canopy shade of a large Chinaberry tree at the end of the village street that exited into the busy area near the store, Davis conducted a thriving business in vegetables, butter, and milk. I have often wondered how he was able to sell milk in such a slipshod fashion and why anyone, except out of ignorance, would have purchased it from him when safe, although higher-priced, pasteurized milk was readily available in the store. Although I remember only one specific episode of Davis's visit to the village, I am certain that there were others. Years later, my father informed me that Davis had regular customers for his milk even in the absence of a careful health inspection system, which then was not a major concern among mill people.

Other peddlers also came into the Old Mill village hawking their wares. In the winter, all of the company-owned houses in the village were heated by wood-burning fireplaces or heaters, and practically all of them, except a few who used kerosene-burning stoves, used wood stoves for cooking. Stove wood was therefore

Alfie Davis, who peddled milk and farm produce in the Old Mill village
(c. 1935). Courtesy of Ewen Hester.

needed throughout the year. Few of the mill hands had free access
to woodlands to cut fireplace wood and stove wood. And even if
they had access to land owned by relatives, few had the means to
transport the bulky split wood to their homes. In time, coal came
to be used in some homes whose residents installed heaters and
purchased this higher-priced fuel. As a result, the mill villages
of the Bladenboro Cotton Mills were a ready market for these
essential products not sold at the company store.

One man who furnished firewood in the Old Mill village was
Dan Cain, who sold stove wood year round. In the early thirties,
Cain, much like Davis, loaded his wagon with stove wood, usually
pine, and "lighter" knots or splinters chopped from the stumps
of long-harvested pines that made easily ignitable kindling, and

drove his mule to the area near the company store where, sooner or later, nearly everyone in the village passed en route either to the store or to work. Even in the Depression years, he had no difficulty in selling his firewood because it was a necessity for nearly every household. According to my father, Cain charged $1.25 for a wagon load of stove wood, which was a very reasonable price when the labor of cutting and splitting and taking it to the village market is taken into account.

In the early thirties, it became a common practice for the company store to stock several boxes of iced-down fish each Friday morning. Sometime before daylight, a truck driver from one of the seafood supply houses in Wilmington dropped off these boxes of undressed spots, mullets, or croakers caught off the Carolina coast. The practice of selling fish, especially on Friday, was not because the mill villagers were Roman Catholics who could not eat meat on Friday. Few, if any, Roman Catholics worked in the Bladenboro Cotton Mills. It was simply because fish provided a cheap, wholesome alternative to beef or pork. One could purchase a pound of fish for ten cents, three pounds for a quarter, depending on the kind of fish. During the summer, fish, rice, cornbread, and iced tea was a common midday meal in the homes of most cotton mill workers. Dinner, as the midday meal was called, was the most substantial meal of the day, larger by far than supper, the evening meal.

The sale of fish at the company store did not prevent fish peddlers from working the village. At least two men come to mind, men who apparently knew well the eating habits of the workers. Blaine Hester, who had four brothers and three sisters working in the mills, was a fish peddler. With a fish box installed on his ancient Ford where the rumble seat had been attached, he visited the Old and New Mill villages in midweek as well as on Fridays. Blanco Formy-Duvall, who was later to become a small downtown shopowner and chicken farmer, also ran a similar fish truck through the village. Nevertheless, workers made most of their purchases at the company store, where the fish on Fridays was both fresh and cheap, rather than buying them off men like Hester and Formy-Duvall, the quality of whose products was sometimes questionable. However, the men who peddled the fish often made a sale to some village residents because of the convenience of purchasing directly from a vendor, because of animosity toward the company store, or because the vendors were relatives. Blaine Hester, for example, was my mother's uncle.

One of the most interesting peddlers, or door-to-door salesmen, was a man named Walter Singletary, a man whom I grew to know better as a teenager because he was a distant relative of my mother. Singletary was a walking genealogical encyclopedia, a man with an extraordinary capacity to remember the kinship connections among all the principal families living in the southern portion of Bladen County—the Smiths, Edwardses, Frinks, Carrolls, Paits, Hesters, Whites, Evanses, Suggses, Bridgers, Kellys. Name a name and Singletary could spend twenty minutes explaining how that individual was related to any other person or family you cared to mention.

Singletary sold Watkins products. Carrying his sample case, he visited the mill villages where he had relatives living. Often he seemed to forget that his business was selling Watkins products. He would sit on a front porch, whiling away the time, talking about this or that person and how he fitted into this or that family. If a sale developed, fine—if not, fine. He had had a good visit, good conversation, and that seemed to satisfy him. From his sample case, Singletary brought a little of the outside world to the villages.

The simple lifestyle of village residents sometimes created a demand for items that are not used today. Villagers rarely covered the pine flooring of their company-owned houses with throw rugs, linoleum, tile, or carpet. To keep these floors spotless, housewives, on their hands and knees, frequently scrubbed them hard with a stiff, strong brush in a solution of lye soap and water until they were thoroughly clean. The floors were swept often, not with a store-bought broom but usually one made of bundled broom straw tied together with a mill-band, a cord used to turn spindles on spinning machines. Straw brooms came primarily from two sources: children of the village who cut the broom straw, made it into brooms, and then sold them door-to-door for a nickel or from peddlers who wandered through the village selling the brooms.

Such a peddler was Sophie Arendt, an elderly black woman who occasionally visited the village to sell her broom-straw brooms. I remember this woman well because of an incident that occurred in the Old Mill village close to our house. After selling her brooms, the old lady was set upon as she left the village by a half-dozen or more mill brats who unmercifully harassed and taunted her, calling her a witch and other vile names. In desperation, she finally reached into a bag slung across her shoulder, drew out a hatchet, and made wide sweeping motions with it at the boys who laughingly harassed her. This torment continued until an adult came on the scene and drove the boys off. Even so, they continued to laugh and call the old woman a witch as she slowly left the village along the sandy rutted street. I don't recall ever seeing her sell brooms again. The harassment of Sophie Arendt was the very first episode of possible racism that I witnessed as a boy.

I say "possible" because later I was part of a similar episode involving an old, ugly, eccentric white woman we knew only as Richardson who lived on the Elkins road near Bladenboro. In passing her house en route to cut reeds in a nearby bay for yard brooms, several boys from the village—I was among them— taunted her with cries of "witch." Richardson's response was a shotgun blast over our heads as we huddled behind an embankment near the road. Fortunately, no one was hit.

Lawn grass was rarely used to cover the small yards surrounding the houses in the Old Mill village. Dirt yards were the rule, and dirt yards had to be swept clean. People took a great deal of pride in having a neatly swept yard. This led to a demand for yard brooms sufficiently strong to sweep up such things as fallen leaves and berries from the Chinaberry trees. The latter, if not swept up, could make an awful mess when they began to decay after dropping in the autumn. The answer was a yard broom made from reeds that could be gathered down near the bays that surrounded Bladenboro. In the summer, a few boys in the village would gather the reeds, tie them with a strong mill-band into small bundles that could be easily managed by a sweeper, and sell them for a nickel or dime in the Old and New Mill villages. The money earned might then be used for ice cream at the company store or possibly a movie at the Lyric Theater in Bladenboro. Such brooms lasted for only a short while and had to be replaced often. With them, one could make beautiful patterns on the ground while sweeping.

There was also some internal peddling in the Old Mill village. Some mill hands cultivated small gardens to supplement their diet and incomes on small plots provided by the mill owners. These gardens were usually located beside or behind their rented village houses. It was not uncommon for a worker whose garden had produced more than his family needed to sell the excess produce to his neighbors. My father remembered that in the fall and spring, Danny Batten, who worked in the Old Mill, always grew more turnips than his family could possibly use in order to sell them to neighbors who ate but would not grow them. Other workers did the same. For those who were ignorant of gardening or who chose not to garden, people like Batten were a source of cheap fresh corn, turnips, collards, beans, field peas, and so on.

There were undoubtedly many other peddlers who visited the Old Mill village and escaped my attention as a small boy. As I reflect on those times, I continue to be surprised that the company allowed such unrestricted access to its village properties. Such openness in the thirties was definitely atypical of southern mill owners. Ordinarily, owners denied or severely restricted access of non-residents to their villages out of fear that they might be troublemakers or union organizers in disguise. What made the Bladenboro cotton mills different? Perhaps its liberal access policy resulted from the owners's astute awareness of the complex family connections in the villages that stabilized their non-union labor force and from confidence in their ability to control disruptive situations that visitors might provoke. And, although peddlers offered some product competition to the company store, it was minor and could thus be tolerated. Nevertheless, for the times the company's allowance of easy access to the villages was most unusual.

Chapter 9

A Question of Status

Every group inevitably develops a pecking order, a ranking of members whose position therein is determined by both formal and informal factors. I found this to be true of workers in the Bladenboro Cotton Mills. Although distinctions of status within the workforce may not have been readily observable to the majority of town residents and local farmers during the thirties and the forties, the distinctions were nevertheless present and discernible to the mill hands themselves. Regretfully, I early concluded that for the majority of local people outside the Old and New Mill villages, cotton mill workers and their families were nothing more than uncouth illiterates who were too much inclined toward violence, the kind of people that they and their children should avoid unless compelled by circumstances to do otherwise. Mill people were all lumped together. This extremely critical attitude blinded outsiders to the diversity and richness of mill life, and it also obscured for them the sometimes subtle deference that workers showed to certain of their fellow workers. Fortunately for many of us whose parents worked in the mills, however, a substantial number of outsiders rejected this harsh, negative assessment of the men and women who worked in textiles.

As a boy living in the Old Mill village, in the summertime I often sat on the steps of our front porch, which abutted the unpaved sidewalk in front of the house. This was a wonderful spot to sit and watch shift changes at the Old Mill, triggered by shrill blasts from a powerful steam whistle half an hour before and on the hour of the change. Installed near the towering smokestack, the whistle could be easily heard throughout the two mill villages and the surrounding area. After the two initial blasts at the half-hour mark, workers stepped out of their houses onto the dirt sidewalk and walked toward the Old Mill. Thirty minutes later, when the final blast on the hour announced the start of a new shift for some and the end of a shift for others, the sidewalk was again filled with moving, tired figures—more bunched together now—headed in the opposite direction toward home.

When the mills were running, this rhythmic, to-and-fro flow of workers occurred daily at the whistle on every village street, all of which remained unnamed. It was one of the constants of life there. Sitting on those steps, I came to know by name most of the passersby on my street, and they came to know me. Often they spoke, and some of them, like my Aunt Clara Tyler (who lived up the street with her husband Daniel—whom we called by the initial D.), frequently stopped and chatted for a few min-

Workers in Bladenboro Cotton Mills, 1932. The author's father, George, is seated in the front row (third from right) next to his brother Major (hand over face). Courtesy of *Southeastern Times*, Clarkton, North Carolina.

utes on the way home from work. Aunt Clara then worked the first shift, which began at six in the morning and ended at two o'clock in the afternoon. Either perched on the steps or seated on the porch of our mill house, I watched this moving band of the men and women who ran the machines of the Bladenboro Cotton Mills.

I don't recall when I first became aware of the kinds of clothing worn by the mill hands, or when I first noticed that a few workers dressed differently from others, or when I first made a connection between clothing and status. This awareness must have come later, after our family had moved from the Old Mill village in 1934 to several different residencies out of the village before settling once again in 1937 in a house in the Old Mill village that

March Of 1932

we shared for a year with relatives. When we left the village in 1938, it was for good. However, our house next to White Oak Original Free Will Baptist Church was less than a quarter-mile from the mills.

From 1929 to 1942, except for brief stints in the Old Mill in the early thirties, my father worked in the New Mill, running the same frames and walking up and down the same aisles for nearly thirteen years. I frequently visited the mills to take his lunch or dinner, depending on what shift he worked, or visited relatives in the villages. My awareness of what mill workers wore at work may thus have developed after I left the Old Mill village. However, in looking years later at two group photographs taken in March 1932 of the men and women composing the spinning and winding departments of the Old Mill and men and women from the New Mill, where my father then worked, I was struck by the accuracy of my memory concerning the clothing they wore at work.

Like my father, a large majority of the men who tended the machines (cards, twisters, winders, and spinning frames) or did other jobs (sweepers, yarn packers, yard work) wore work clothes purchased at the company store. For many of these workers, this store was the only source of such merchandise because only it extended credit based on the hours already worked. Their attire was therefore determined by the limited supplies available at the store. On the job, their typical clothing was a blue denim shirt (long-sleeved or short-sleeved, depending on the season), overalls or blue jeans (that is, work pants), brogans, and sometimes a cap. The men were generally a scraggly dressed group; it was clear from their ill-fitting and drab clothing that they wore whatever was available. In short, they dressed without much regard for style or appearance.

In the Depression years of the thirties, there was as little luxury of choice about work clothing as about other areas of life. Except for top wear in the winter, and except for long or short sleeves, there were few seasonal changes in work clothes. And, of course, even if there had been greater clothing options available, the warm and lint-filled work environment of the mills, particularly in the summertime, greatly discouraged any serious thought among the men about upgrading their dress.

Among female workers, there was also a sameness of quality in dress imposed by the times and the nature of their work. During the warm seasons of spring, summer, and fall, most of the women who worked in the spinning and winding rooms of the Bladenboro Cotton Mills—the departments where most women were assigned—wore what appeared to be collared, homemade cotton-print dresses that were comfortably cool and easy to wash. There was a variety of print designs on the fabric. Sometimes they wore dresses of solid colors made of a similar cotton fabric. Once I recall seeing my Aunt Clara, who was a small, wiry woman, returning from work wearing a blue cotton dress with a side pocket in which she carried a small, very sharp red knife for cutting ends. And frequently their clothing was a mixed bag. Like their male counterparts in the thirties, it appeared that while working in the mills, female workers generally wore whatever was available. Other than the impact their working dress had on their social relationships with other workers, male and female, the clothing of women in the mills had no effect on status. Their clothing did not reflect official status or a position of authority that caused others to show them deference. There were no female bosses or supervisors. Other than Mrs. Margaret (Maggie) Bridger, one of two members of the mill-owning family who managed the finances of the company store, I do not recall any woman in a position of authority in the Bladenboro Cotton Mills during the thirties and forties.

It was different for the men; dress clearly reflected their power status in the mills. For example, when Joe, Charley, or R. C. Bridger, owners who took a direct hand in management, visited the works from their downtown offices or the office at the end of the Old Mill, they were very conspicuous because of their clothing. In the summertime, this usually consisted of a white short-sleeved shirt, a necktie, and dress pants and shoes. In the winter, it might be a suit.

Workers reacted to their presence in different ways, depending largely on which owner was touring the mill. Joe Bridger, who was president of the mills before his death in the forties, was a tobacco-chewing older man who was aloof, gruff, and unapproachable. Behind his back, workers referred to him as "Old Man Joe." Workers kept a respectful distance from him. R. C., a much younger man who took over the presidency when Joe died, had played in the mill's ball club and had much greater rapport with the mill hands. He was therefore much more approachable than Joe. For example, because the mills were not unionized, my father and a small delegation selected by their fellow workers visited R. C. in his mill office to complain about the unfair distribution of work between workers on different shifts. Prior complaints to a department supervisor had not corrected the problem. Thanks to R. C.'s intervention on behalf of the men, within twenty-four hours the issue had been rectified. Nearly all the workers knew the owners, and the owners knew many of them. Except for Joe, it was not uncommon for an owner walking among the machines to recognize a worker by a nod of the head, by a wave of the hand, or by speaking to him directly—but contact rarely went beyond this cursory recognition.

But many of the men avoided contact—even eye contact—with a visiting owner by hovering ever closer to their machines—as if suddenly their work had become so demanding it required their immediate and undivided attention. Not until the owner had passed was there a lifting of eyes to follow him down the rows of machines as he left their work area. This form of reaction, however, was most evident among female workers in the spinning and winding rooms. Perhaps they were more aware of their vulnerability to the power that a visiting owner had over them. Other workers were satisfied with repeated, quick glances at the moving figure as they continued their work. As a mark of deference and respect, if for any reason an owner stopped and spoke briefly to a worker (and this was not uncommon as younger members of the mill-owning family replaced the older generation), the latter unfailingly addressed the official as "Mr. Charley," or "Mr. R. C."

Except on the company-sponsored baseball team, where mill workers and several younger sons of the mill-owning families played and associated freely with a sense of comradery, there was rarely any social contact among workers, owners, or their family members. It would have been extraordinary for one of the sons of a mill-owning family to openly date or have out-of-school social contacts with the daughters of mill hands or for the sons of mill hands to have open social contacts with the daughters of the mill-owning families. Nor was there a likelihood of social interaction among the adults who lived in these two different worlds. The physical distance between the mill villages and Front Street, the "Street of Beautiful Homes" where the owners lived, was about one mile, but the social and psychological distance was incalculable. The deference of employees and the social distance between them and the owners were conditions that both parties recognized and accepted. There was no appreciable change in this situation until after World War II, when veterans returned to the villages with new perspectives and attitudes about relationships.

Workers showed the same deference to the mill superintendents. Superintendents were usually very experienced men, some with college degrees in textiles from such institutions as North Carolina State College. If they had no degrees, they nearly always made up for the lack with years of experience in cotton mills throughout the region. Like the roving owners in the workplace, the superintendents of the Old and New Mills were conspicuous by their dress, which was similar to that of their employers. The white shirt and tie, khaki pants, low-quarter shoes rather than brogans were standard dress. In the summer when mill interiors were warmer than usual, the shirt might be worn open. Theirs was a familiar presence in the mills as they walked about directing and coordinating the flow of work with lesser supervisors, huddling first in one department of the mill and then in another as they conferred with their underlings about the quality or the rate of work. In some respects, their power over workers was even greater than that of the owner because they directly supervised their work and were authorized to hire and fire. Consequently, in the Bladenboro Cotton Mills, where there was no protective union to speak for the workers, many of them feared the superintendents, his assistants, and overseers more than they feared the infrequently seen owners because they held the livelihood of hundreds of men and women immediately in their hands. Mill hands were therefore unusually circumspect around the superintendents.

Even so, some of these officials were highly respected and admired because of their fair treatment of the workers. My father remembers that once, when my mother was very ill, we were living alone in a four-room house in the Old Mill village because a family that had occupied two of its rooms had recently moved. One of his fellow workers complained to Superintendent Smith about his family occupying such spacious accommodations and requested permission from the superintendent to move into the empty portion of the house. Knowing of my mother's illness, Smith rejected the request. The rooms remained unoccupied until my mother's sister Marybelle, her husband, Dave, and their daughter, Alma moved in—tenants who were far more acceptable than the one who had made the initial request. My father was always grateful to Smith for showing him such consideration. I suspect that there were other cases in which a mill superintendent's authority was used to benefit workers. Nevertheless, that authority was feared by the mill hands, whose jobs were essential in the Depression years of the thirties.

The elevated status of the superintendents was evident in another conspicuous manner. Their housing, when provided by the owners, was distinctly different and separate from that of the workers who lived in the villages. For example, the superintendents resided in a painted house situated west of Bladenboro on Highway 211 across from the gasoline storage tanks of Walter Elmore, a local distributor of Cities Service gasoline. Located several hundred yards from the west end of the New Mill and about the same distance south from the company-owned dwellings of workers in the New Mill village, the residence was superior to any occupied by employees and their families. Unlike the houses in the villages with their outdoor privies, the superintendent's house had interior plumbing and running water. The same was true of the assistant superintendent who, in the early thirties, lived with

David J. and Marybelle E. Pait who, with daughter, Alma, shared our four-room company house in the Old Mill village in the early thirties (c. 1930). Courtesy of George G. Suggs, Sr.

his family in a company house in the Old Mill village near the company store.

Furthermore, these officials and their families were the sole occupants of their dwellings. In contrast, a number of employees with small families often shared a house, two families—often related—occupying a dwelling of four rooms. On at least three occasions my parents shared such a residence, first with my Aunt Clara and Uncle D. Tyler, then with my Aunt Marybelle and Uncle David Pait, and finally with my mother's Aunt Evelyn and

Uncle Seth Hester. The living space was extremely limited and cramped in such an arrangement. Furthermore, until the sixties mill houses remained unequipped with indoor plumbing; until then each had its conspicuous outdoor privy. From time to time these toilets would be relocated to a new site, a task that was relegated to one of the few black workers then employed by the mills.

Water used for drinking, washing, and cleaning was obtained in buckets from a hand pump found in the median of the streets, a pump that was usually shared by several families in the early days of the villages. As late as the early thirties in the Old Mill village, my family and those of Solon Ludlum, Tully Singletary, John Pait, David James Pait, and others used the same hand pump for household water. Later, additional pumps were added and positioned to serve the residents of only two houses. The superintendent and the assistant superintendent of the mills, of course, were not subjected to such inconveniences because of their position, power, and status, all of which may have caused their underlings to feel uncomfortable in their presence.

In addition to the superintendent and his assistant, the owners employed an overseer for each of the major departments within the Bladenboro Cotton Mills. The carding, spinning, winding, and twister rooms of the Old and New Mills had either an overseer or an assistant overseer for the day and night shifts, someone to be directly in charge in the absence of the superintendent. The assistant overseer usually worked the night shift. The owners generally selected men from the ranks to fill these positions. The more ambitious workers aggressively sought these jobs because to be appointed an overseer was a significant advancement involving more pay and recognition. Furthermore, to be an overseer enhanced the possibility of moving on to a similar position or even a better, higher-paying position in one of the many family-owned mills in southeastern North Carolina. Such mills were found in nearby Lumberton, Whiteville, Rockingham, St. Pauls, Raeford, Wilmington, and Fayetteville—all within a seventy-five-mile radius of the Bladenboro Cotton Mills. Men with limited education but a demonstrated talent for successfully managing cotton mill workers were in high demand in the many mills found in the region even in the Depression years of the thirties. Consequently, there was a high turnover rate among overseers, who exploited their mobility.

In making their choices for these positions, therefore, the owners factored in several considerations—potential ability to supervise men and women, demonstrated knowledge of the work in a particular department, intelligence, and the number of family members employed in the mills. The latter was important because overseers who had large, extended families working in the mills were less likely to leave for another position. Roy Davis, Jetter Hester, Byron Bullard, Bob Hester, George Hester, Fred Williams—all became overseers of various departments, or "rooms," in either the Old or New Mill after working as regular employees. Nearly all of them had been section hands, or "fixers," before their promotions.

Upon assuming the position of overseer, a change of dress and attitude, although not necessarily of old habits, immediately occurred. Off went the overalls and on went the belted khaki pants, usually a white shirt, and shoes a step above brogans— changed clothes for a new position. The changed status from worker to overseer did not necessarily mean a change of residence. Most of the men remained in the same company housing. Of the men mentioned above, for example, George Hester, Roy Davis, and Fred Williams continued to reside in houses in the Old Mill village. Others did likewise. However, residence in one of the villages was not a requirement of the position, for Bob Hester, Jetter Hester, and Byron Bullard lived elsewhere—close by the mills but elsewhere.

Now endowed with the ability to hire and fire, an authority transmitted downward from the superintendent, an overseer was in the position to make life either easy or difficult for former colleagues, friends, and relatives. Some of them did not hesitate to use their newly acquired power to favor family members in work assignments or to coerce others into doing their bidding. For example, Bob Hester, one of my mother's uncles who became an overseer in the Old Mill, used his position to aid family members under his supervision with jobs and favorable work assignments. This practice often caused discord among other workers under his control. Hester was often vindictive, even to those persons related to him through marriage. In a work dispute with my father over broken promises to let him run a set of frames, Hester caused him to quit, temporarily separate from his family, and successfully seek work in nearby St. Pauls. Only the intervention of a sympathetic superintendent, the same superintendent who had earlier helped my father with the housing, made it possible for him to return and obtain a new position in the New Mill under another's supervision. It was such arbitrary use of power that caused many workers to fear the overseers, men with whom they had formerly worked closely, more than the superintendents or the owners.

Sometimes several members of the same family became overseers, creating a small nexus of power and influence that extended into nonwork areas like religion. For example, George Hester and Bob Hester were brothers and overseers in the Old Mill—and also members of the White Oak Original Free Will Baptist Church. Many members of that church, including my father, worked in the mills, some directly under George or Bob. Because they were a large family, the Hesters dominated the congregation and Bob Hester, the oldest of the clan, dominated the family group. This allowed him to have an extraordinary influence on church policy, particularly in the selection of ministers and other officials. Contributing significantly to his influence in the church was his position in the mill, from which the church sometimes benefitted. Through the Hester overseers, for instance, successful requests were made to mill officials for financial assistance in reroofing the sanctuary. Consequently, many nonfamily members who disagreed strongly with Hester on religious issues often deferred to him because of his power in the workplace and his ability to obtain aid from the mill owners for church projects.

Below the overseers, there was another category of workers in the mills called section hands, or "fixers." Unlike the overseers, their enhanced status had nothing to do with the power to hire and fire. These were men who had a recognized talent at fixing things, and their job was principally to keep the machines running. There were scores of machines, and they were in constant need of repair. For each shift in each department, a fixer was on hand because a machine that was down was a nonproductive machine. Although fixers were paid slightly more, reflecting their skill level, the messy nature of their jobs precluded the wearing of different clothing to indicate this difference.

Nonetheless, many rank-and-file workers admired the mechanical ability of the fixers and recognized their position as being one step above that of simply operating the machines. To be a fixer in the spinning room, for example, was to be recognized as one who possessed a superior knowledge of the machines and hence a greater knowledge of the spinning process. Furthermore, it was not uncommon for the owners and the superintendent to select an overseer from among the fixers. The position was thus recognized as one from which advancement could occur.

There was another class of workers who were accorded a higher status in the workplace than fixers because of their mechanical and technical skills. This group consisted of machinists and electricians who operated out of the machine shop of the mills. They ran the lathes, drills, banding machines, and other equipment that created on site the gears, axles, bars, rollers, and other items needed in the operation of the mills. They also did the electrical repair work needed throughout the mills. Except for the person in charge of the shop, none of these men had managerial responsibilities over other workers, unless it was an assistant on a particular job. Even so, they represented an elite group within the workforce of the mills. Of the men I knew who worked in the machine shop, only Clarence Butler had a college degree. When he left to pursue other opportunities, he was replaced by two men—Charley Kinlaw and his brother Talley—who had been taught their trade on the job. The same was true of Bill Hester, an electrician for the mills. Although among the most highly paid of the workers, the status of such men was not reflected in the clothes they wore. As I remember, they typically dressed in the same work clothes as the other mill hands. Nevertheless, many workers often deferred to them because of their esoteric skills and because their jobs permitted them an enviable degree of freedom and movement that the others, who were bound to their machines, did not have.

Among the jobs held by the rank and file, there were several that were less desirable than others—jobs that made running spinning frames or carding machines look very appealing. Within the mill itself, one such position was that of sweeping in one of the departments. This was a dirty, unhealthy job that required close contact with lint and dust stirred up by the broom. It was the job of the sweepers to keep the floor free of the lint that was constantly falling throughout the mills in spite of overhanging humidifiers that emitted a find mist. After collecting the waste on large burlap sheets, the sweepers tied and carried the bundles off to the waste mill, where the sweepings were again introduced into the production process. Under the best of circumstances this would have been a terrible job, but in the thirties, when there was not much concern about a healthy work environment, the conditions were appalling.

Another reason the sweeper's job was so unpleasant—even dangerous—was the use of tobacco products, then very prevalent among cotton mill workers. Because of the fire hazard, no one was allowed to smoke cigarettes or cigars in the mills. However, there were no on-the-job restrictions on chewing tobacco and dipping snuff. Some addicted workers always kept a cylindrical box of Society or Tube Rose snuff, a bladder of Railroad Mills, or a plug of Black Maria or Days Work in their overalls bib, in their work aprons, or on their machines. They daily indulged in the unwholesome pleasures of dipping and chewing while busily tending their machines. This practice necessitated expectorating somewhere, and the release usually occurred at the end of a spinning frame, against a support beam in the mill, or around the drinking fountains, where the mouth could be easily washed out. The area around the frames of the heavy chewers and dippers was often encrusted with an ever-growing accumulation of expelled, dried tobacco juice, so much so that occasionally it became necessary for someone to chip the mess away. And the areas around the fountains were often so filthy that one drank at one's own risk. It was the responsibility of the sweeper to clean up the unsanitary mess that many dippers and chewers daily deposited in the work environment. Sweeping was therefore not a job that any sane person really wanted because it was a dirty, nasty job that raised the threat of contracting tuberculosis or other lung diseases that plagued cotton mill workers in the twenties and thirties. Consumption, as tuberculosis was then commonly called, was dreaded by everyone who worked in a cotton mill. Naturally, the status of anyone simpleminded enough or desperate enough to take the job of sweeper was not very high. Rather than sweep, some individuals chose not to work.

There was at least one mill job that engendered less status than the sweeper. The residents in the mill villages relied entirely on outside privies, making it necessary for someone to periodically dig new holes into which the accumulation under the outhouses was drained. Because of the large number of workers and houses in the villages, this was a job that needed to be done frequently. In the early thirties I remember that this loathsome work was done by black men, among the few Negroes employed by the Bladenboro Cotton Mills until after the Second World War, when blacks were gradually incorporated into the workforce—first on the yards, moving heavy bales of cotton into and out of cotton warehouses, and then into the less desirable, dirtier jobs in the mill such as sweeping and working in the lint-filled picker rooms.

I recall that when I was a young boy of four or five, Richmond Johnson, one of these black men, saved the life of Harvey Ludlum, a friend my age, when he fell into an open pit into which the contents of an outhouse had just been drained. Without hesitation, Johnson reached shoulder-deep into the maggots and excrement, grabbed Harvey, and pulled him to safety. Neither was a pretty sight afterward! If mill officials later bestowed any reward or public recognition for Johnson's unselfish and heroic rescue, I don't remember it. However, the Ludlums owed the life of their son to him.

Author with playmates Floyd Pait (left) and Harvey Ludlum (center) in Old Mill village (c. 1933). Courtesy of George G. Suggs, Sr.

I do recall that one black, despite his race, enjoyed unusual status because of his association with Joe Bridger, the president of the Bladenboro Cotton Mills. Bridger lived on Front Street in one of the largest and finest homes, surrounded by trees and flowering shrubs that required a gardener for upkeep. For this job he selected a black man called "Shorty," who lived on the premises. Shorty was a dwarf with an infectious grin, a man liked by nearly everyone—white and black—in Bladenboro. In addition to maintaining Bridger's yard, he was also a watchman at the mills when they were shut down on the weekends and holidays. Shorty and Waitus Hester, a white man, shared this responsibility—one watching the Old Mill, the other the New Mill. Although being a watchman was not a cushy job, it was a step above that of digging pits and moving outdoor toilets. Shorty therefore enjoyed a status much greater than the other blacks, who worked in low-status jobs around the mills before the late forties. Everyone recognized the fondness of Bridger for this short black man, which undoubtedly helped to make him more acceptable to the other white employees. When he was on duty as a watchman, he rarely received any guff from anyone in the villages—despite his color.

Among the workers who ran the machines, there appeared to be little status differentiation based solely on the kind of machine that one tended. Although one might have a personal preference of machines to operate, in terms of status it made little or no difference whether one operated a spinning, winding, carding, or twisting machine. As long as the work was performed efficiently, it certainly made no discernible difference to the supervisors concerning who operated what. As I have previously noted, however, women employees were generally found running spinning and winding machines because management had apparently concluded that their nimble fingers were best for tying ends, not because these positions were thought to be of higher or lower status.

Whatever status rank-and-file workers might acquire among their companions usually resulted from activities outside the workplace. For example, there were several Protestant churches scattered around the mill villages that many workers attended— "Holy Roller" churches, as they were often derogatorily called. Some employees became leaders in these churches, serving as superintendents of Sunday schools, church treasurers, or Sunday school teachers. Responding to the "call," some mill hands went into the ministry, working at their machines during the week and preaching the gospel on Sundays—usually in the more evangelistic or holiness churches. Several such men come to mind— Gaston Hester, Luther Smith, and Holland Hughes. Within the workplace, fellow members of their congregation generally accorded them greater respect and deference because of their pastoral positions and religious activities.

And several workers were wonderful storytellers, which helped their status. When the mills were shut down on the week-ends or holidays, these men would sit and regale workers with story after story. Such a man was Bud Edwards, who later opened a small store near the Old Mill on Highway 211. Such men were also held in slightly higher esteem by their fellow workers but not because of their jobs in the mills.

Status also accrued to outstanding athletes who played on the company's baseball team, the "Spinners." Mill hands loved baseball. As a result, they greatly admired and even made heroes of local players who excelled at the game. John Lee Hammond, for example, was better known and respected because of his prowess as a powerful hitter and skilled fielder. There were others as well who are discussed in chapter 11.

As I recall, union activity was minimal in the Bladenboro Cot-ton Mills throughout the thirties and forties and, consequently, had little to no impact on relationships or status. Nevertheless, the mills were not totally immune to the massive labor upheaval that beset major textile centers like Gastonia, North Carolina, in the great strike of 1934. Nor were the mills located in towns like Lumberton, which in 1934 had four operating mills. Rather than recognize the United Textile Workers Union and negotiate a contract, the Lumberton owners shut down their mills, leading to the ultimate demise of two of the four mills. It was during the labor troubles in Lumberton that union organizers from there attempted to organize the workers in Bladenboro.

This attempt at unionization occurred when I was a youngster of nearly five. Although I was too young then to understand the seriousness of the labor troubles that resulted from the union's efforts to organize, I nevertheless have vivid memories associated with the unrest because our company house was located not far from the east end of the Old Mill, where the company's on-site office was situated. On one occasion, hand in hand with my father, I joined a crowd of workers milling about outside the office area. It was an orderly crowd that respected a rope fence that kept strikers a short distance from the mill itself. I don't recall any angry speeches or loud, boisterous threats emanating from the workers or mill officials. And I am certain that my father did not consider the situation dangerous or he would never have taken me to the scene. However, in later discussions with him about this memory, I learned that there was indeed trouble, serious trouble.

As he recalled the episode, the trouble between labor and management originated in the demand of workers for a wage increase. Union organizers from Lumberton, seeking to exploit the growing dissatisfaction over wages, arrived and attempted to organize the mills. Some of the disgruntled employees wanted to join the union, but others did not. And, of course, the mill owners were strongly again unionization. Consequently, the issue over wages became quickly embroiled in the union question, which led to a strike and the crowd noted above. Following minor disturbances, local and county police officers arrived to maintain peace and order and to prevent an outbreak of violence. They were not entirely successful.

According to my father, one evening after dark as mill officials were consulting together in the office of the Old Mill, someone standing on the Seaboard Railroad (which ran parallel to Highway 211 and the mill) fired a rifle shot through the office window. A story quickly circulated that if an official near the window had not stooped to retrieve an object off the floor at the precise moment before the shot was fired, he would have been struck by the bullet. Next day, amid much confusion, a worker named Giles Guyton was apprehended and charged with the act, causing some workers who expected further violence to purchase ammunition for their guns. Fortunately, this violent episode and the expectation of further violence caused both sides in the dispute to become more serious about reaching a settlement, which was concluded that very day. The workers received a small increase in wages; however, they agreed to remain nonunion as the owners wanted. My father was convinced that "if a settlement hadn't been reached, somebody would have been hurt." Fortunately, no one was. Thus the Bladenboro Cotton Mills, located on the far periphery of the massive labor troubles erupting throughout the textile South in 1934, did not entirely escape the agitation of that era.

For the remainder of the thirties, neither my father nor I remembers any major labor troubles in the mills nor any attempts to organize the workers. From time to time there were disagreements between labor and management but these were quickly settled. About two years after my father left the mills in 1942 for wartime work in the Wilmington shipyards, an issue over wages led to a walkout of some but not all mill employees. A load of wartime orders and no available labor replacements predisposed mill officials to resolve the conflict as rapidly as possible, but not before acts of vandalism occurred. In a beautification effort before the walkout, the company had planted oak seedlings on the streets of the villages and alongside Highway 211 in front of the mills. During the course of the disagreement, many of these seedlings were pulled out of the ground, never to be replaced.

Sometime during the course of the walkout, Joe Bridger, then president of the mills, addressed a small crowd of striking workers from a platform near the mill office. As I recall, the meeting was marked by much grumbling among the assembled men and women as Bridger, a rather gruff individual, attempted to find out exactly what their complaints were. Unorganized and without a skilled spokesman who could clearly articulate their grievances, the meeting degenerated into muffled demands for more money from unidentified individuals in the crowd who were clearly reluctant to be recognized as leaders of the group. R. C. Bridger, who later replaced Joe as president, then spoke to the workers. Younger and more in touch with them because of his close association with the company's prewar baseball club, R. C., as I recall, appealed to the crowd's patriotism by reminding them that a war was in progress that required everyone to work together and produce as much as possible for the war effort. He also asked that in the future workers come to him with their grievances before striking, and he promised that mill officials would listen and try to resolve their complaints to everyone's satisfaction. Not long afterward, the walkout ended.

With his release from the Wilmington shipyards following the end of the war in 1945, my father returned to the Bladenboro Cotton Mills for a while before leaving again to work in the shipyards in Newport News, Virginia. Because of the poor allocation of work by a supervisor on preceding shifts, he and other workers on his shift were often sent home for lack of work or put into the position of being unable to make production. Joined by several fellow workers, my father took the matter directly to R. C. Bridger, now the president of the company, and explained the situation. Fulfilling the promise he had made earlier to striking workers, he dealt with the complaint immediately, ordering the supervisor to correct the situation without delay. Of course, my father was impressed by the quick resolution of a problem that had affected his wages.

The last labor difficulty in the forties that I observed occurred in the summer of 1946, when I worked temporarily in the packing room of the New Mill. It was not serious as labor disputes sometimes are. One day I became aware of a growing silence as machines were shut down and then an increasing commotion on a nearby loading platform outside the mill's winding room. My curiosity aroused, I looked out a window and saw approximately twenty-five women, winders and spinners, noisily moving about and looking expectantly toward the door from which they had just exited. Soon Byron Bullard, an overseer, appeared and began to address the women. From where I stood observing the scene, I could not hear what Bullard said to them. But within minutes the walkout was over as they began a movement back into the mill and started up their machines. I later learned that the brief strike had originated in increased workloads that the women considered to be unfair. When a few bolder ones shut down their machines and walked out in protest, others followed suit in spontaneous support. Bullard apparently resolved the women's complaint because there were no further work stoppages.

Organized labor never established itself in the Bladenboro Cotton Mills—not before, during, or after the thirties and forties. The company was nonunion throughout its existence. My father and I often speculated about why this was so. His explanation was simple: in his opinion, the workers simply did not think that a union was necessary. He himself didn't think one was needed, even when he had grievances. Like him, many of his fellow workers had entered the mills straight from the farm and carried with them their long-held agrarian attitudes of individualism and suspicion toward outsiders, whom they generally considered to be troublemakers. Furthermore, many workers took their cue about unions from the owners and management of the mills, who naturally opposed unionization. Although at times these officials were seemingly distant and unapproachable, as a rule they did not deliberately harass or oppress their workers. And during the hard times of the Depression, they were the means of survival for many workers, providing them extended credit at the company store when it was not available elsewhere and providing most of them with limited work even when there were few orders for yarn. But a major reason that organized labor failed to make inroads in the Bladenboro Cotton Mills was its geographic isolation from the larger centers of the textile industry, perhaps making it not important enough to merit a major effort and expenditure of union resources. Whatever the reasons, the mills were never organized. Consequently, organized labor played no role in determining status relationships within the mills.

Within the mills and in the villages, there were all kinds of people—good people, bad people; violent people, peaceful people; religious people, irreligious people; ambitious people, nonambitious people; lazy people, hardworking people; intelligent people, unintelligent people; saintly people, sinful people; drinking people, teetotaling people; lovable people, unlovable people. Each mill hand and villager knew where he or she and all the others fitted in these categories; each knew how much status one's authority, skills, morality, character, ability, or position entitled one to have. Unlike the outsiders' perception that mill workers and their families were all alike, the reality was complex and finely tuned. Like other groups, mill workers established their own pecking order based on multifaceted—often intricate—life experiences.

Chapter 10

EARLY EDUCATION IN THE MILL VILLAGES

MY FIRST AWARENESS of education outside the home occurred in the fall of 1933, when my family lived in the Old Mill village next to the John Pait family. Learning that a preschool had been established in the village, my mother, with the strong support of my father, decided that I should be enrolled there. My registration in this school, created exclusively for children of mill workers, revealed to me for the first time my mother's strong interest in education. Because of the early death of her mother, she had not finished high school (she later earned her diploma when she was in her mid-fifties). She was determined that her children should "get" all the education possible. It was a message that I heard repeatedly over the years. The daughter of a sawmill operator, my mother was eighteen in 1927 when she married my father, a mill hand with a fourth- or fifth-grade education. He took her to live in a company house in the village; it was then the best that he could offer her. Self-conscious about his own lack of schooling, he always strongly supported my mother's determination to provide their children with all the education that they could afford.

My mother never felt comfortable living in the mill village. Although many of her mother's people lived in nearby company houses, she yearned to leave. She longed for a place of her own out of the village. Unlike many residents there, she refused to accept the notion that her children were destined to become mill workers, that working in a cotton mill was the only occupation open to them. She saw education as the way "out." I later learned that she was not alone in this view. Many mothers in the villages were equally determined that their children should escape the mills.

My venture into formal education was a memorable one. Reluctant to leave the security of home, I resisted the more peaceful means of persuasion my mother employed until, kicking and screaming, I was nearly dragged along a dirt street of the village to the "school," which was located at the end of an unnamed street adjacent to the company house of Roy Davis, a cousin of my mother. Along the way, I received gentle but firm encouragement from my mother, who applied a switch across my bare legs, a switch taken from a large chinaberry tree that grew in our backyard. The stinging blows set my legs to dancing and moving forward toward school. When it came to education, I discovered, my mother was a very determined woman.

The school met in a house in the Old Mill village provided by the Bladenboro Cotton Mills, one of the company dwellings that normally housed two small families. It came to be partially supported by subsidies and agricultural surpluses provided by Franklin D. Roosevelt's New Deal, which was then in its formative state. As I recall, other than a number of extra straight-backed chairs, tables, and a wooden fence surrounding the house, there was nothing to distinguish it from the numerous other dwellings in the village. There was certainly no comparison to a modern school. Nothing had been done to make it a delightful place for children to learn. None of the rooms was freshly painted. Nor do I recall bookshelves loaded with childrens' books or any learning aids. Each room was lit by a single lightbulb on a cord dangling from the ceiling. Like all the other dwellings, the house had no indoor plumbing. Outside was a single, substantial outhouse, with the boys and girls each having a two-seater section divided by an interior wall. If there was any playground equipment, I don't recall it. The physical facilities were—I think even for the times—drab.

Nevertheless, the school was important in the lives of the children whose parents insisted they attend. We were four- and five-year-old mill children who were accustomed to having little or nothing; many of us then paid little attention to the starkness of the facilities. After all, what was there was very similar to what

George G. and Carrie E. Suggs, parents of the author, during the fifties when father worked in the Newport News shipyard. Courtesy of George G. Suggs, Sr.

we knew at home. None of us knew that better existed. And, too, this was not a school that focused on the academics. We were too young for such things. Our forays into academics consisted of crayons and paper and not much else. Here our preschool experience was directed at helping us learn things that we needed to know, practical knowledge that some of us had not received at home.

To illustrate: our two teachers, whose names I have forgotten, paid much attention to personal hygiene. Over and over they stressed to us how important it was to wash our dirty hands with soap and to keep our fingernails clean. Dirty hands and fingernails were common to mill children, especially boys, because there were no lawns on the village, only frequently swept dirt yards. A favorite game at that time, even among children attending the preschool, was marbles—a game that put one on one's hands and knees in the dirt. And in the summer, probably the coolest place to play was in the cool dirt under the high porches found on some of the houses like the one our family occupied with my Aunt Marybelle, Uncle Dave, and their daughter, Alma. In the absence of interior plumbing, water had to be lugged into houses from pumps. In short, what with one thing and another, keeping children clean was difficult. But in these preschool sessions, our teachers attempted to inform us about the importance of personal cleanliness. Such lessons were continued thereafter in the primary schools where, after pledging allegiance to the flag, fingernail inspection was the next item on the day's agenda.

Another point of focus was oral hygiene. Like most children of four or five, most of the children with me in the fall of 1933 knew or cared very little about the importance of brushing their teeth. And based on my observation of their mill parents, many of whom were prodigious users of tobacco and whose teeth consequently showed the destructive effects of the product, I doubt that many of the children had encountered a toothbrush before attending the preschool. Our school not only supplied us with toothbrushes but our teachers worked diligently to teach us how to use them. I remember our standing around in clusters of three or four while they demonstrated the use of the brush and told how important the teeth were to our good health.

Another vivid memory involved cod liver oil. Every so often, our teachers lined us up for a teaspoon (or was it a tablespoon?) full of the substance. We each had our personal spoon that we had brought from home. Some unknown person had determined that we needed to be regularly dosed with the terrible-tasting stuff. Although I do not remember hearing my parents discuss any widespread occurrence of rickets among mill children that necessitated a supplementary intake of vitamin D, there must have been some explanation for this practice. Perhaps some pharmaceutical company somewhere had built up a huge inventory of cod liver oil and its officials had persuaded their counterparts in public health that dispensing it to us was a healthy way to reduce the surplus. Whatever the reason, "cod liver oil time" created an enormous distaste for the oily substance.

Sometime in the summer or fall of 1934, our family moved from the Old Mill village to my grandfather Asie Suggs's farm, located several miles north of Bladenboro on Highway 131 toward Dublin. Even then my mother arranged for me to attend the kindergarten, which met in a different and larger house in the Old Mill village. Several days a week one of the two teachers, Miss Evelyn Thompson, who lived further from the village than we did, commuted to the school. En route, she stopped and permitted me to ride with her. So although I no longer lived in the village, I continued to attend the mill school because of the generosity of this lady. More children attended this next level of schooling, which seemed to be far better organized than the previous one.

Our teachers continued to emphasize personal cleanliness. Lessons in washing hands, brushing teeth, combing hair, and cleaning fingernails were a daily occurrence. Contests were held to find the persons with the cleanest hands or the cleanest fingernails. And once there was a contest to determine which boy came to school with the best-combed hair. Eugene Williams, brother of Odel, won this contest when he arrived at school with his normally unruly, cowlicked hair doused in a sweet-smelling, oily tonic

that forced it into perfect place along the part line he had cho-
sen. He had a thoroughly plastered look. It was a winning look,
of course, that received much attention from our teachers—but
not many of his friends admired a head of hair so saturated with
tonic that tornadic winds could not disturb it. This emphasis on
cleanliness was difficult because the only water available, as at the
other school, was water from a nearby pump.

Although there was little recreational equipment available,
we nevertheless enjoyed our recesses at this school. When we
went out to play, we found nothing to compare to the items found
on a modern school playground or city park—no slides, no balls,
no monkey bars, no high or low bars, no balance beam, no basketball hoops. None of that! The few pieces of equipment on our playground had been fashioned at the mill carpentry shop, probably
by Archie Pait, who followed his father in supervising the shop for
many years. Our swing set consisted of several swings made from
plow lines and wooden seats suspended from an overhead beam.
There was a seesaw or teeter-totter, also locally made, that consisted of several lengths of dressed two-by-ten lumber resting on
something like a low, extended workhorse for a fulcrum. There was
no other equipment. Nevertheless, when released onto the small
backyard where the equipment was located, we joyfully played on
these limited, crude facilities. It made little difference to us that
the equipment was anything but fancy. Occasionally there were
accidents resulting in minor hurts and injuries. Once a playmate
was painfully hurt when her hand was mashed between a loose
board being used as a seesaw and the fulcrum. And there were
the occasional hurts from the bumping and shoving that occurred
because of the confined area of the schoolyard. But during my
stay at this school, no one was ever hurt sufficiently to require the
services of a doctor.

During holidays such as Thanksgiving and Christmas, our
teachers attempted to broaden our range of experiences. Christmas of 1934 was marked by a school program built around the
season. A few children had participated in church-related programs that required individual performances before an audience,

but most of us had not. In preparation for the program, to which parents were invited, the teachers handed out recitations to be learned and practiced, taught new Christmas carols (religious and secular), and made us rehearse and rehearse and rehearse! Most of the recitations were scriptural, having to do with the birth of Christ. I was asked to memorize a passage from Luke 2:8–14, verses that I have never forgotten. I recall that my mother insisted that I go over and over these verses until I had committed them to memory. Others were given similar passages or poems to memorize. On the day of the program, parents came and sat in straight-backed chairs while we went through our renditions of verse and song. As I recall, it all turned out very well. The teachers were pleased and, of course, the parents gloated in the performance of their children.

In retrospect, I suppose that the mill preschool was comparable to the Head Start preschool programs of today, which are designed to help underprivileged children. However, some parents in the village (including my own) would have resented the notion that their children fell into such a category because times were then difficult for everyone. I have always considered myself very fortunate to have had the opportunity for two years of preschool experience before entering the first grade in 1935 because, as I recall, at the time North Carolina did not have a preschool program in its public schools. My mother was right to insist that I take advantage of the opportunity that the village preschools offered. They started me on a journey that eventually ended with a Ph.D. from the University of Colorado.

Chapter 11

BASEBALL:
THE SPORT OF MILL WORKERS

WITHOUT A DOUBT, baseball was the sport that gripped the interest and imagination of workers in the Bladenboro Cotton Mills from the twenties through the forties, as it did for most Americans in this period. Boxing was perhaps a distant second. Partly responsible for their fascination with baseball, of course, was their lack of access to news about other sports that so dominate radio and television today—sports like basketball, football, golf, and tennis that, had they been available, would have offered other options. Especially during the Depression years, only a few families in the villages had radios. They were a luxury beyond the means of most mill workers. But perhaps more important in making baseball dominant was the presence of a local team called the Spinners that participated enthusiastically in a vigorous textile league, a team that was sponsored and underwritten by the company for labor and public relations purposes. And, of course, the Bladenboro High School also fielded a team each spring called the Bulldogs. The success or failure of the baseball Bulldogs was the subject of much conversation. Furthermore, the presence in nearby towns, such as Lumberton and Fayetteville, of Class C and D farm clubs of major-league teams also helped to sustain the workers' interest in baseball. The exploits of these minor-league clubs were passed on by workers who moved often from mill to mill and by relatives who came to visit.

My introduction to baseball occurred one Sunday afternoon in the summer of 1933, when I was nearly four. Our family then shared a house with my Uncle Dave, Aunt Marybelle, and their daughter, Alma, in the Old Mill village next to the John Pait family and across the median and two sandy rutted streets from the families of Solon Ludlum and Tully Singletary. After lunch my father and I were sitting on the front steps of our mill house watching several older boys bat and catch a baseball on the streets and the median separating the two rows of dwellings that fronted each other. The area was totally unsuitable for a game of any sort, much less a game of throwing and batting about a baseball capable of smashing the windows of nearby houses. However, with no playgrounds or recreational areas to service the mill villages, it was not unusual for the children of workers to use the streets for play, especially on the weekends when the mills were shut down and automobile traffic was nearly nil.

One of the boys at play was Garland Stubbs, a tall, skinny teenager who was later to play on the company's ball club. He was at bat when a friend of my father joined us on the steps. They had been engaged in conversation for only a few minutes when Garland hit a hard line drive that smacked me squarely in the pit of the stomach, knocking the wind completely out of me. Distracted from the game by his conversation with his friend, my father had failed to protect me from the blow, although I was sitting directly in front of him. When I finally was able to get my breath and bawl with the pain, my father, angry as much at himself as at the boys, promptly put an end to the game. Garland and his friends, who were clustered about and frightened at my state, were delighted to leave the premises because they apparently had concluded that the errant ball had seriously hurt me.

Four years later, in the spring of 1937, the love affair that mill workers had with baseball became more evident to me. After having moved from the Old Mill village for a while, our family had returned to a different part of the village and shared a house with my mother's Uncle Seth, Aunt Evelyn, and their two children, across the street from my Aunt Clara and her husband Daniel, who also shared a rented house. One family, with two boys whose names I do not recall, lived behind us in another company house. Unlike most families in the village, this one had a portable radio that they generously shared with their neighbors on the weekends. On Saturday and Sunday afternoon during baseball season, they would bring the radio out on the porch and listen to games that were being broadcast. In time a half-dozen or more men and boys gathered on the porch, a chatting, changing group whose members came and went after cheering on their favorite player or team. With the mill shut down for the weekend, the radio broke the silence that prevailed over that part of the village. On Saturday evening after the games were over, another group of villagers would gather to listen to the Grand Old Opry from the same radio.

On any weekend, Azzie Hardin's downtown barbershop would be filled with mill workers. During ball season, the conversation there was certain to be about baseball. There were two shops in Bladenboro for whites, Azzie's and one run by Charley Bell Ward. Azzie's place was the choice of the majority of mill hands, while Charley Bell's shop drew clients principally from the town residents and farmers in the area. The difference in the clientele of the two shops produced a remarkable difference in their social atmosphere. At Azzie's during ball season, the radio was usually tuned in loudly to whatever game was being broadcast, provoking loud, sometimes boisterous, laughing and talking from customers when something exciting happened in the game and bringing absolute silence with situations like—score tied, two out with bases loaded in the last half of the ninth inning, a favorite hitter for the home team at the plate with three balls and two strikes, and the game hanging in the balance on the next throw from the pitcher. As a boy I often sat in Azzie's shop on Saturday afternoon soaking in this obsession of mill workers with baseball. In contrast, over in Charley Bell's shop, I later learned as a young man, the atmosphere was quieter, the silence occasionally broken by subdued conversation among the waiting customers about crops, fishing, and sales.

Before 1943 the home games of the mill baseball club were played on the diamond of the local high school, which was located less than two miles from the cotton mills and villages. This field was surrounded by a wooden fence, which, when I became aware of it, was badly in need of repair. Fans attending the games sat in a covered grandstand that offered some protection from the sun and rain. (I have been told that this facility was built in the late

1930s, together with the adjacent high school gymnasium, as a project of the New Deal's Works Progress Administration [WPA] and the Public Works Administration [PWA]). There were no individual seats for the spectators, who sat wherever they desired. The grandstand was built over the players' dressing rooms, which consisted simply of cramped space and benches—no showers, no lockers. Visiting team members usually showed up in uniform and went directly to the dugout, which was really not a dugout but only an open bench designated for the visiting team on one side of the grandstand. The home team occupied the other bench. Although I attended few games in this old stadium, I was in it often when the Spinners or the high school team practiced. I remember vividly the crack of the bat on balls and the way the sound bounced off the old wooden fences. To see the games, a few friends and I usually climbed up on the back of Mosley Page's barn shed near the field, from which we had a clear view over the fence, and watched the game from there.

Unfortunately, as dusk fell on a late summer day in 1943 during the Second World War, the grandstand, the gym, and the fence surrounding the park caught fire and burned to the ground. At the time this did not surprise me because a lot of trash and paper had accumulated underneath the grandstand. Once the fire was going, the pine lumber burned intensely, making it impossible for the local volunteer fire department to put out the blaze. There was not to be another ballpark with a grandstand in Bladenboro until after World War II, when the Bladenboro Cotton Mills built Spinners Field northwest of the New Mill village.

Often my father and others told stories about certain workers they knew who had played on the Spinners team while in their twenties and early thirties. These men had become local heroes to their fellow workers, who were often thrilled at the players' exploits on the diamond during hot Saturday afternoons. They were remembered—often for specific outstanding plays against a rival team—long after their playing days were over. It was not uncommon during conversations about baseball, which occurred frequently in those days on the weekends when idle workers sat around smoking, chewing tobacco, and whittling, for someone to remind his listeners about an extraordinary catch, a crucial hit in a tight game, or a fine pitching performance by one of these men. Consequently, even after their playing days were over, they enjoyed a comradery with their fellow workers that few could match. Their status was as nearly like the sports heroes on the national baseball scene—the Babe Ruths, the Lou Gehrigs—as local players in the Bladenboro Cotton Mills could ever achieve. Having played well for the mill team made them very special in the eyes of many of their fellow workers, and the former players enjoyed their local celebrity.

Several of these exceptional players were veterans of World War I who had returned from overseas duty in France to resume work in the Bladenboro mills. Once back from military service, these men remained in the mills for the rest of their working lives. Although playing baseball on the Spinners team was undoubtedly a poor substitute for the excitement of service in a faraway land, it certainly added a bit of zest to the otherwise drab existence of their working fans in the stands. Of course, as they grew older they gradually left the team and became simply employees. But even after age had forced an end to their baseball careers, their fellow workers perpetuated in stories their on-the-field exploits, further enhancing their reputations as superb players. How many times have I heard someone say: "I'm tellin' you what's the truth. If thet feller had hada chance, he coulda played in the major leagues! He wuz thet good." And who knows? Maybe some of these talented players of the twenties and thirties who played in the textile league that included the Spinners could have done so—that is, if they had had the chance to demonstrate that talent in the right places before the right people.

I came to know several of these men who had played for the Spinners team in the late twenties and early thirties, so the stories I heard from my father and others about their talents and exploits on the baseball diamond were credible to me even though the men had aged considerably. Two of them were brothers—Azzie and Oak Hardin. Azzie was a veteran of the war; Oak was not.

When I came to know them in the late thirties, Azzie owned a barbershop, which was located in Bladenboro in quarters rented from James Albert Bridger. Azzie was my barber for many of my growing-up years. His brother Oak continued to work in the mills. They followed these occupations until they retired. One would not have concluded from the later appearance of the brothers that they were the stuff of local legend. The same was true of Otto Thompson who, when I first came to know him, was tending a small farm for a brother-in-law near Bladenboro. Nor would one have guessed that Jess Lewis, who worked in the mills when I knew him, was once an excellent ballplayer. Time had altered those characteristics that had made them stellar players. My father also told stories about two other men whom I never knew—Corley Williamson and Cauley Fields—who, from his standpoint, played extremely well for the Spinners. These men and other players remained in Bladenboro for the rest of their lives and were enthusiastic supporters of local baseball teams.

During World War II, the Spinners went into hibernation for the duration of the conflict. But immediately after the war in the late forties, mill management restored the team, and it became a member of a revived textile league in southeastern North Carolina. R. C. Bridger, then the president of the mills, took enormous interest in the resurrected ball club, seeing that it was properly equipped, arranging released time from work for its members to practice and play, and securing a coach and several key players needed by the team. Furthermore, he showed his commitment to the team by having the company build a new ballpark and stands called Spinners' Field on the west end of the New Mill village. Although reestablishing the team was obviously designed to fix the loyalties of employees and make them less amenable to the appeals of union organizers, which were then beginning to circulate among the workers of locally owned mills in southeastern North Carolina, nevertheless mill hands and their families thoroughly enjoyed the baseball games at Spinners' Field.

Spinners' Field was superior to the facilities that burned in the summer of 1943. Although its grandstand was made of wood like that of its predecessor, Spinners' Field was newer and its diamond was properly maintained by mill employees. It was surrounded by a metal fence and, as in many other parks that were built in the immediate postwar years, lights were eventually installed so that games could be played at night. Its dressing rooms were also much nicer than the crude ones at the other site, with lockers and showers. In a reversal of the practice of the prewar years, the Bladenboro Bulldogs crossed town to use the facilities of Spinners' Field, not only for baseball but also for football, especially for scheduled night games. Spinners' Field remained an important sports arena for the community until the management of the Bladenboro Cotton Mills began to dismantle the Old and New Mill villages by disposing of the houses in preparation for selling the company. Today the ballpark site is occupied by low-cost housing.

Before these developments could even have been foreseen, however, the majority of team members lived in these villages and worked in the mills. Several younger members of the mill-owning Bridger family also played for the Spinners, for example, brothers Levy and Charles Bridger, who were excellent athletes. Levy, who pitched and played first base, was as smooth a fielder as I have ever seen. And for a while in the late forties, W. A. Hough, principal of Bladenboro High School, was catcher for the team, and the coach was a man named Columbo, who coached baseball and other sports at the local high school. Several out-of-towners, hired for summer work in the mills because of their baseball ability, also played. They did little work. Local players who were regular mill employees included such men as John Lee Hammond, Garland Stubbs (who had practiced his craft on my stomach years earlier), James Cain, William Hester, and Earl Hughes. Some of these players had unusual abilities. For example, William Hester, who had a very strong arm, could hurl a knuckleball—a difficult pitch to throw—from the outfield into the infield. Other than for the attention it generated, I have no explanation for his performing this feat.

Perhaps the most memorable of the mill players on the Spinners team in the immediate postwar era was John Lee Hammond, a tall, broad-shouldered, powerfully built individual who looked every inch a ballplayer. He swung a powerful bat and played well in the infield. John Lee, who could hit a baseball a country mile, liked to demonstrate his hitting prowess during batting practice. He insisted that the pitcher throw the balls where he could use his great strength to pound them out of the park or send them sizzling through the infield, a form of hitting that pleased his fans and onlookers.

After graduating from high school, one summer I joined the Spinners *very* briefly as a pitcher, and on a hot afternoon it was my lot to pitch to John Lee during batting practice. Knowing how hard he swung at every pitch and fearing a line drive directly at the pitcher's mound, which could have torn my head off, I deliberately threw the ball so that I knew he would have difficulty hitting

Bladenboro Spinners Ball Club at the new Spinners' Field. John Lee Hammond stands in back row, third from left between brothers Charles and Levy Bridger (c. 1950). Courtesy of John Lee Hammond.

it—fast and inside. John Lee became terribly frustrated and angry at not being able to slam each pitch out of the ballpark. More concerned about my safety than his ego, I endured his anger rather than run the risk of being injured by a bullet-shot off his bat.

During the late forties, John Lee was one of the few players on the Spinners team who attracted the attention of the professional scouts who prowled about the Carolina textile leagues looking for talent. A scout from a major-league team with a Class D farm club in nearby Lumberton invited him there for a tryout, making him something of a hero among the mill workers. Everyone who knew him was confident he would succeed; everyone who knew him wanted him to succeed. Unfortunately, he apparently blew the opportunity, although not from lack of ability. According to stories that later circulated to explain his failure, although he had done well and showed promise while in Lumberton, John Lee was so disappointed at the low salary and so terribly homesick for Bladenboro—only thirteen miles away—that he left the team and returned home to family and friends, returned to work in the mills and to play ball for the Spinners. Although his supporters were disappointed to see one of their own fail to make the grade in professional ball, they nevertheless were happy to have him playing again for the home team, where he continued, of course, to excel. With John Lee swinging a bat, the team's chance of winning was greatly enhanced.

With the revival of sports in the postwar years, Bladenboro High School also fielded a baseball team that drew much support from the mill workers. In the spring of 1946, while war restrictions on gasoline and other scarce items were still in effect, the Bulldogs emerged again to play teams from neighboring schools. As a member of the high school team in 1946 and 1947, I remember that the largest number of fans, standing back and parallel to the baselines on the field where the old grandstand had stood before it burned, were workers from the mills. (This was before the building of Spinners' Field northwest of the New Mill village.) Some individuals, such as H. B. Hargroves, who had a minor connection with the mills, showed great interest in the school's sports program during those difficult times. R. C. Bridger, then a highly placed official of the Bladenboro Cotton Mills, regularly refereed alone all the school's football games. Once when a baseball game was scheduled with nearby Evergreen and our transportation failed to appear, H. B. Hargroves arranged with the Grover Pait trucking firm for the team to be transported on a flatbed truck to and from the game—certainly a rather dangerous way to travel but the only means then available!

Among the sports-minded workers in the Bladenboro Cotton Mills, baseball was clearly the sport that ranked number one. A weekend visit to Azzie Hardin's barbershop during baseball season easily confirmed this conclusion. With the shop radio tuned in to whatever major-league game was being broadcast, customers, who were principally from the mill villages, talked of nothing but baseball while waiting for an empty chair. And in other favorite gathering places of younger mill workers (for example, Pelo Lockamy's poolroom near Azzie's shop), the subject of conversation was likely to be about baseball. For nearly four decades during the heyday of the Bladenboro Cotton Mills, baseball remained the sport of choice among the workers there.

Chapter 12

MILL HANDS AND RELIGION

FOR MANY WORKERS in the Bladenboro Cotton Mills, religious commitment played a significant role in determining the style of their everyday lives, causing them, for example, to refrain from using alcohol and tobacco; to avoid all movies at the downtown Lyric Theater; to reject personal adornments such as lipstick, rouge, rings, bracelets, and earrings; to wear only the plainest of clothes; to avoid such pleasures as dancing; to abstain from using profanity and obscenities; and, generally, to live exemplary lives of austerity. In the minds of such workers, their religious convictions forbade the enjoyment even of harmless, simple pleasures, such as drinking Coca-Cola or Pepsi. Of course, the demanding hard times of the Great Depression and the stressful times of World War II helped to encourage this ascetic behavior by making religion an appealing, welcome sanctuary in troubled times. In their distress, they gravitated toward those religious denominations that preoccupied them with extraordinary behavioral demands on their lives.

Members of the denominations who followed the above strictures were totally convinced that sin and evil lurked everywhere and had to be resisted. There could be no yielding. In their view, they must constantly guard against succumbing to the powers and temptations of the devil, a powerful being whose aim was to damn their souls forever in a fiery hell. They never questioned the reality of the devil, nor did they question his causal role in the hard lives they were living. Escape from his clutches was to be found in living exemplary, blameless, moral lives, a salvation revealed in their conduct, behavior, and strict adherence to their religious convictions.

During the thirties, other workers in the Bladenboro Cotton Mills lived lives that were very similar to their more religious-minded fellow workers—but for entirely secular reasons. Religious convictions had little, if anything, to do with the similarity of lifestyles between the two groups. And neither an admiration for the ascetic, devout life nor a desire to imitate it produced the similarity. The similarity was caused primarily because there was no money in the pockets of most workers for tobacco or alcohol, no money for personal adornments, no money for stylish clothes, no money for entertainment, no money for anything but the bare necessities. Until the outbreak of World War II, when the federal government created job opportunities with higher pay in its massive, widespread rearmament programs in such nearby places as Fayetteville's sprawling Fort Bragg and Wilmington's shipyard, life was precarious in the matter of finances for most families dwelling in the Old and New Mill villages. Yet those who sought meaning and comfort in their religious faith contributed much to the style of life in the mill villages.

Workers in the Bladenboro Cotton Mills who attended church belonged exclusively to one of the several Protestant denominations that had made inroads in the area around the mills. There was no Roman Catholic church in Bladenboro, no Mormon church, and no Jewish synagogue. In the absence of Catholics, Mormons, and Jews, there was no need, of course, for such places of worship.

Perhaps the most prominent working-class church was the West Bladenboro Baptist Church, located, as the name implies, on the west side of town and the north side of the Old Mill village. From the twenties through the forties, West Bladenboro Baptist, as it was called, was a conventional wooden structure, cooled in the summer by raising the windows, and heated in the winter by a potbellied stove. It was here that the bulk of Old and New Mill villagers who were Southern Baptists worshiped. The church was conveniently located within easy walking distance from any point in either of the two villages.

For many years, the Reverend Lorenzo Todd was the pastor of

West Bladenboro Baptist Church, where many working families of the
Bladenboro Cotton Mills attended services (c. 1940). Courtesy of
Bladenboro Historical Museum.

West Bladenboro Baptist. From time to time, several of his sons
worked in the mills. I remember Reverend Todd very well because
of the manner in which he addressed an opening day session at
Bladenboro High School in the mid-forties. After being introduced by Principal A. A. White, he went through five minutes of
nasal "thank yous," thanking everybody: White, the faculty, the
students, members of the county board of education, residents of
Bladen County, the citizens of Bladenboro—everyone he could
think of—for the opportunity to speak to the students on this
occasion. I also saw him often during the summer because West
Bladenboro Baptist, like other churches in the area, often hosted
"singings": choirs and quartets from various churches would gather
for an afternoon of religious music. As minister of the host church,
Reverend Todd was a conspicuous figure at the singings.

Although there was another Southern Baptist church located
not far away on Front Street in Bladenboro itself, few employees

of the mills attended services there—possibly because the Bridger families, who owned the mills, were its most influential members. It is likely that some mill hands concluded that while they would tolerate the deference expected of them in the workplace, they would not tolerate it in their worship services; they went to the more conveniently located West Bladenboro Baptist, where they felt more at ease with working-class people like themselves whose lives they shared daily.

Nevertheless, among mill employees who did attend services at the First Baptist were the Foster Smith and Henry Freeman families, both of whom lived within the town limits—the Smiths on Back Street, the Freemans on Railroad Street, which connected Front and Back streets. Both families lived within easy walking distance of the First Baptist Church. Foster Smith worked as a supervisor in the mills; Henry Freeman, commonly known as "Hen," worked as a bookkeeper who managed the mill payroll. Of course, by virtue of their positions, these men were not of the rank and file. Not until well after the Second World War, when the Bridger families sold their interests in the mills and their children departed for other places and professions, did the number of older mill employees joining the First Baptist Church (for example, my parents and Ed and Lula Skipper) actually increase.

There were two other Southern Baptist churches near town: Zion Hill, located about two miles to the north toward Dublin, and Galeed, located about two miles south toward Chadbourn. These churches were not working-class churches because their membership consisted principally of small landowning farmers. However, some mill hands and their families attended these churches. My Uncle Major Suggs and his family attended Zion Hill Baptist Church until the fifties when, after some dispute among the members of the congregation, they moved their membership to the First Baptist Church in Bladenboro. Although the membership at Galeed Baptist Church was also principally composed of small landowning farmers, some of its members worked in the mills—for example, M. J. Skipper (who also did some farming) and his family.

Within half a mile east of the mills on Highway 211 was the White Oak Original Free Will Baptist Church, a wooden structure whose framing of heart lumber had been supplied by my maternal grandfather, Charley Edwards. Although a Baptist church, White Oak, as it was called, was not Southern Baptist. Like West Bladenboro Baptist, White Oak's membership consisted primarily of mill workers and their families. Thus it was a predominantly working-class congregation that assembled each Sunday for religious services. For many years, White Oak was my parents' church—until the late fifties, when conflict among its members over various issues caused my parents to transfer their membership to the uptown First Baptist Church.

The most dominant family in the life of White Oak were the Hesters, particularly the sons of Daniel and Exie Hester—Bob, Seth, Jim, Blaine, and George. My maternal grandmother, Fannie Edwards, was the sister of these men. Most of the many children of these brothers and several of their sisters worked in

White Oak Original Free Will Baptist Church, the family church of the author, who stands off the right shoulder of the tall girl dressed in white located front and center (c. 1940). Courtesy of Marie Wilson Phinney.

either the Old or the New Mill. Bob and George were supervisors there with the authority to hire and fire. Consequently, through them members of the extended Hester family found jobs in the mills and, more often than not, membership in White Oak. The domination and control of church affairs by Bob, the oldest Hester brother, reflected his power and position in the mill. His brothers and sisters deferred to him, their working children deferred to him, his underlings at the mill deferred to him, and he expected all members of the White Oak congregation to do the same. A spiteful man given to drink, his in-church behavior was at times comical, cynical, and pathetic.

Although White Oak's was a working-class congregation, there were several members who did not work in the mills or who both worked in the mills and farmed. Graham Wilson, a good man who managed the dry goods department of the Bridger Corporation Store in Bladenboro, his wife Ada, and daughter, Marie, had no connection with the mills, yet they were among the most faithful of White Oak's members. Marie went on to become a missionary in Asia and Latin America. Kelly Pait was a farmer who bicycled to White Oak each Sunday until the arrival of his mail-order bride. Harry Pait, a relative of Kelly who also farmed, was a member. Leroy Brown, who combined work in the mills with farming and David Hester (no relation to the Hesters named above), a farmer, were longtime faithful members of White Oak. Nevertheless, mill workers and their families, particularly the Hester clan, dominated the membership of White Oak Original Free Will Baptist Church.

Within a stone's throw of West Bladenboro Baptist Church was another working-class sanctuary: the Fire Baptized Free Will Baptist Church. It was situated near the fork of a road that split the Old Mill village. The fork skirted both the Old and New Mill villages, curving westward by the future site of Spinners' Field and through Bridger farmland to join Highway 211 west of the mills. The church was of a different denomination from White Oak Original Free Will Baptist Church—it placed greater emphasis on "holiness" in daily life. It was this church and two other

Author standing with younger brother, Charles, and father outside house next to White Oak Original Free Will Baptist Church (c. 1940). Courtesy of George G. Suggs, Sr.

local churches (the Emmuel Holiness Church, located across the Seaboard Railroad tracks in front of the New Mill, and the Church of God, located on Highway 211 about half a mile west of Bladenboro) that taught their members that in order to defeat the devil and assure their salvation by holiness and godliness, they must deny themselves the pleasures of alcohol, tobacco, dancing, movies, sex outside marriage, and personal adornments such as rouge, lipstick, rings, and necklaces. Only by doing so could they escape the clutches of the devil and avoid eternity in hell. Of course, other churches (including our own White Oak Church) stressed this same lifestyle of denial but to a lesser degree. The membership of the Fire Baptized Free Will Baptist Church, the Emmuel Holiness Church, and the Church of God consisted principally of mill people who lived in the nearby villages.

The worship services at the Fire Baptized Free Will Baptist Church were always lively, with much loud singing, shouting, praising, speaking in tongues, and hellfire-and-damnation exhortation from the minister. The nature of the services naturally attracted curious teenagers like myself who, I am sorry to say, were more interested in the spectacle than in the salvation of our souls. The revival meetings in the spring and fall at this and other holiness churches especially drew us into the back pews to observe the extraordinary energy that members employed in their worship. The sight of the good brothers and sisters writhing and rolling on the floor in religious ecstacy, leaping up and down while speaking in tongues, bawling unashamedly at the altar while others prayed loudly to God on their behalf, or fainting (either from the release of their sins or exhaustion) was enormously exciting for teenagers to watch. The extremely emotional upheavals that converts in these churches underwent in seeking forgiveness and salvation probably accounted for their willingness to conform to the strict behavioral demands of their denominations. Sometimes the pursuit of salvation extended these services late into the night, at times making it extremely difficult for workers on the morning shifts to be on time.

Another church existed in the very heart of Bladenboro, located between the Bank of Bladenboro and the Lyric Theater. This was the Presbyterian Church, an old wooden structure that was replaced in the sixties by a smaller brick sanctuary that was relocated across the tracks of the Seaboard Railroad to a site on Front Street. The members consisted primarily of the families of town residents like Dr. S. S. Hutchinson and small local farmers like Frank Davis. Weather permitting, as late as the mid-forties Davis, his wife, and their teenage children (who lived west of the Bladenboro Cotton Mills) rode a mule-drawn wagon two miles down Highway 211 into town for Sunday morning services at the Presbyterian Church. Although it was not a church that usually appealed to mill people, some of them were members there. Three of my father's sisters, Clara Tyler, Mae McLamb, and Kate Davis (with her husband, Foster, and daughter, Hazeline) attended services there. All three sisters, my paternal aunts, worked in the mills as spinners, while my Uncle Foss, as Foster was called, worked as a frame hand. For whatever reason, they felt more at home in the Presbyterian Church than in those churches where their fellow mill workers held positions of influence and authority.

Only two of the above churches were able to support full-time ministers—the First Baptist Church and the West Bladenboro Baptist Church. Robert Hall served as minister at the former for years, while Lorenzo Todd did likewise at the latter. Because the mill-owning families were influential members who gave First Baptist their strong financial support, it was not unusual that the church employed a resident minister who had the luxury of a parsonage. However, it was unusual that West Bladenboro Baptist, a working-class church, employed a minister whose sole profession was the ministry. In the other working-class churches noted above—and even the small Presbyterian Church—the practice was to have bimonthly "preaching" services because the congregation could not financially support a resident minister. For example, at White Oak Original Free Will Baptist Church, which my parents attended for nearly three decades, over the years a series of preachers (for example, Griffin, Anderson, Johnson, Mallet, Jernigan, Wooten, Cheshire) was "called" to preach by the congregation. They came, some from as far away as Anderson, South Carolina, expecting to receive only room and board and whatever might be garnered from a "free will" collection at the end of their sermons. Sometimes they received very little. My father recalls hearing the Reverend Anderson make a humorous appeal to the congregation shortly before the collection was taken. He requested at least enough money "to buy a tank of gas and to put a little grease in my rear end" for his trip home. Because of the hard times of the thirties, money was always in short supply at White Oak, which, I think, was typical of all the churches.

Occasionally, some churches benefitted from the emergence of homegrown preachers who resided in the mill villages or on their periphery. It was not extraordinary for mill workers, especially if they were members of the more evangelical churches like the Fire Baptized Free Will Baptist Church, to feel the "call" to enter the ministry. More often than not, they lacked formal education beyond high school, and some had never attained even a high school diploma. They entered preaching believing that God would supply whatever message He wanted His people to hear. Like many members of their working-class congregations, these men did not believe that an educated ministry was necessary to preach the word of God.

When the Original Free Will Baptists established a college at Mt. Olive, North Carolina, to provide preministerial training and to educate the young people of their denomination, there was only lackadaisical support from the White Oak congregation—even some resistance. Few held the view that one ought to be educated to serve as a Christian minister. I once heard a tearful plea for financial support for this new college from the Reverend Millard Johnson, who had helped to found the institution. The plea fell on many deaf ears. In the minds of some, all that a potential minister needed was to experience a legitimate call. While I was a teenager, several workers in the mills responded to the call, leading them to preach on Sundays.

Among the mill workers who responded to the call to preach were two young men with established families from the West Bladenboro Baptist Church—Gaston Hester and Holland Hughes. Luther Smith, who was a member of the Fire Baptized Free Will Baptist Church, also heard the call. When the call came to these three men, they were employees of the Bladenboro Cotton Mills, where they continued to work in the early years of their ministry. With the passage of time, their success made it possible for them to devote themselves full time to preaching, or at least to leave the mills. Luther Smith, for example, successfully combined his ministry with being a small-time entrepreneur, operating a small store, acquiring and renting houses, and developing land for sale. Gaston Hester, who in the early days of his ministry continued to live in the village while working in the mill, eventually devoted his entire time to preaching. Holland Hughes continued to work in the mills and preach until time and ill health ended his career. Occasionally the children of mill workers also felt the call. In the early fifties the call to ministry came to James Hester, the youngest son of my mother's Uncle Jim Hester. James became a successful Baptist minister who served churches around Bladenboro for decades. These homegrown preachers with mill connections helped to alleviate the shortage of ministers and make it possible for the poorer churches to employ resident pastors.

The presence of significant numbers of mill people in a congregation often worked to the advantage of working-class churches. Their officials occasionally petitioned the management of the Bladenboro Cotton Mills for assistance when, for example, church repairs were needed. On one occasion, I recall that the congregation of White Oak Original Free Will Baptist Church appointed a delegation to approach Joe Bridger, then president of the mills, to request a donation to help reshingle the leaky roof of the sanctuary. As I recall, Bridger complied with the request of the committee. It is probable that other working-class churches near the mills made similar episodic requests and that mill officials granted them when possible to do so.

What impact did the workers' involvement in religious affairs have on the public's perception of textile workers as a group? Unfortunately, the mill hands and their families who lived exemplary lives because of their religious convictions were not the deciding factor that determined how mill workers were viewed by residents of Bladenboro and the farms around the mills. At best, in the thirties and forties that perception was generally negative and unflattering. To unknowledgeable outsiders, the mill people, separated to the west of town in two villages composed of rented company housing, seemed to have coalesced into an unwholesome, close-knit group whose members were all the same. Outsiders made little distinction between the "good" and the "bad" residents of the villages. The result was that, with the possible exception of workers who lived outside the villages and engaged in other occupations like farming, mill people generally felt ostracized from the rest of the community. Exacerbating this alienation and isolation were the frequent stories that circulated locally about fights and brawls, shootings, and excessive drinking in the villages—stories that seemed confirmed when, on Saturday nights, the local jail in Bladenboro would be filled with drunks, including men who worked in the mills, picked up by the town marshal.

There was much truth to some of these stories. For example, my father recalls a night in the early thirties when John Jackson shot Joe Taylor in the Old Mill village. Taylor, a heavyset, middle-aged man who lived next door to our family, served as a deputized marshal in the villages, the person who was responsible for maintaining order among the residents. At the time, Jackson had a well-earned reputation as a criminal, a man capable of anything. Consequently, nearly everyone was afraid to antagonize him; nearly everyone sought to avoid him for fear that he would do them bodily harm. Jackson's shooting of Taylor directly involved my father, who was asked by Taylor's wife to rush to Bladenboro for a doctor. Taylor, who bled badly from the wound, subsequently died. In an earlier violent episode, Jackson had shot through a living room window and seriously wounded a man with whom he had had a minor disagreement. And on another occasion, he had fired off an indiscriminate shotgun blast and shattered glass jars under my father's house. News of such incidents circulated among nonmill people and shaped their views about textile workers.

Some of the villagers were also overly fond of their liquor, which they managed to buy in spite of little money. Their tendency toward excessive drinking may have been caused by the hard times and the harsh work environment of the mills, which was very stressful. Whatever the reason, when they drank alcoholic beverages, they drank not just to be social but to become drunk. Often they wandered into town, where the local sheriff quickly arrested and incarcerated them. The drinking and resulting violence engaged in by a few mill hands smeared them all. The presence of a large number of churchgoing workers who lived clean, responsible, moral lives was more than offset by an irresponsible few who, unfortunately, determined the public perception of textile workers in the Bladenboro Cotton Mills. This fact was recognized by the more responsible village residents, some of whom, like my mother, made getting out of the village a prime goal in life. Although they recognized that the negative view of them held by many outsiders was inaccurate, biased, and unfair, they felt helpless to do anything except separate themselves from it.

Although religion may not have been the deciding factor in influencing the public's general perception of workers in the Bladenboro Cotton Mills, it was certainly highly influential in shaping the individual lives of the men and women who worked there. On Sunday mornings around nine o'clock, weather permitting, church members and their children left their homes for the often long walk to Sunday school and a preaching service. I remember as a small boy walking through the Old Mill village and along Highway 211 to attend services at the White Oak Original Free Will Baptist Church. My parents and I were not alone, for there were other families en route either to White Oak or to other churches. Among them were some of the finest, most moral people who ever lived. Religion was a dynamic force in their lives, helping to make them what they were—an enduring and patient people who met adversity with great faith and courage.

Chapter 13

THE COMPANY STORE

NEXT TO THE church and the workplace, the most vital institution in the lives of workers in the Bladenboro Cotton Mills was the company store. A rectangular brick structure located west of Bladenboro at the east end of the Old Mill and the north edge of the Old Mill village, the store sat on a triangular plot closely wedged between Highway 211 and a siding of the Seaboard Railroad that ran parallel to the mill. Its plate glass storefront faced the highway and its rear, the railroad siding and the village. At times, cars and trucks sped by the store, endangering workers who milled around its front, especially during the two o'clock shift change, while boxcars and hopper cars—either empty or loaded with boxed yarn and coal—rumbled and banged away at its rear, blocking movement of village residents to and from the store as a steam locomotive positioned the cars for loading or unloading. As a result of train and vehicular movement, the area surrounding the store was very hazardous. A teenager was killed directly in front of the store when hit by a car; and another youngster was similarly killed where the railroad siding cut diagonally across Highway 211 near the store.

Opened in the early thirties, the company store was originally staffed by experienced salesmen drawn from the Bridger Corporation Store in Bladenboro, an establishment that catered to the general needs of town residents and farmers in the area. Among the clerks selected was Emmett Guyton, a veteran of World War I, whom the mill owners chose to manage their new enterprise. Guyton, who had grown up on a farm off Highway 242 north of town, was a member of a well-known, long-established family in the southern portion of Bladen County. Before he became manager, he and his brother Dewey had combined farming with retail work at the Bridger Corporation Store. To be closer to his new position (but yet a respectable social distance from the mill and its villages), Emmett built a brick home for his wife and two daughters, Thelma and Eunice, beside Highway 211 immediately west of town, the only brick residence between the town and the mill. For more than a quarter-century, he managed the company's store, working behind the counters alongside his clerks. Even so, youngsters like myself, who lived in the Old Mill village at the beginning of the store's history, knew that Mr. Emmett was in charge. He wore the symbol of authority in those days—a white shirt and a tie. In recognition of his position as manager and as a mark of respect, I always called him Mr. Emmett as instructed to do by my father, who enjoyed a good relationship with Guyton.

The company store was not a large operation. Located in a building approximately forty-by-eighty feet, it carried items most in demand by mill families—staples like flour, lard, sugar, salt, canned goods, rice, dried beans, milk, and meat, and dry goods like bolt cloth, pants, shirts, work shoes, and overalls. When you entered the store from the front, on the right there was a soda fountain, a glass showcase for candy, a sturdy wooden counter that concealed pull-out bins of bulk sugar, rice, and beans, and wall shelves loaded with canned goods, cigarettes, and snuff. Running nearly the length of the store on the left were showcases where dry good items were displayed and shelves loaded with bolts of cloth, blue denim shirts, overalls, and other items. In the center near the first support beam was a showcase that displayed an odd assortment of items (for example, knives, harmonicas, and yo-yos) that seemed rarely to change. Occupying the rear was a large showcase for fresh meats, principally pork and beef, behind which were a chopping block and a walk-in freezer for storage. To the left of the showcase near the back exit was the store office, which coordinated its activities with the on-site office of the Bladenboro Cotton Mills located in the nearby Old Mill. There was nothing fancy or frivolous about the company store. With wooden floors and canopied lightbulbs dropped from the ceiling, it had an atmosphere as basic as the commodities that were sold there. It was clearly designed to serve the essential needs of mill workers with limited incomes.

Central to the operation of the store was the small office in the rear that was managed by Miller Bridger and Margaret Bridger, two members of the mill-owning family. Miller worked in the office until his death in an automobile accident and Margaret until her retirement. At one time or another, nearly every worker in the Bladenboro Cotton Mills stopped at the office window to conduct business with either Miller or "Mrs. Maggie." Because the mills paid wages every two weeks, the usual business of the worker was either to borrow against future earnings (if he were in debt) or to obtain advances against unpaid labor in order to purchase goods in the store. Whether borrowing or drawing against accumulated earnings, the worker received the company's fiat money—Maggie's gold. A prim lady who treated everyone kindly and respectfully (even youngsters like me who were occasionally sent by their parents to perform these transactions), she issued the coins as directed by her associate, Miller. After the loan of Maggie's gold had been properly recorded for later deduction from the worker's wages, he used the coins to purchase items in the company store or spent them in Bladenboro, where some town merchants accepted but discounted the coins for their goods or services. When I visited the store as a boy, it seemed to me that there was always activity around the office window as workers, their wives, or their children transacted business there.

Visiting the store was quite an experience for a young boy. When we lived in the Old Mill village in the early thirties, our rented house was located near the store on an unnamed dirt street that emptied into the space immediately behind it. Although only four or five years old, I often visited the store alone to make purchases because of my mother's illness. My father, who trusted me with such tasks, instructed Mr. Emmett and Mrs. Maggie to give me whatever I asked for, whether grocery items or Maggie's gold, and charge my purchases to his account. Consequently, I visited the store often—sometimes with my father, sometimes alone. After our family's temporary return to the Old Mill village in 1937 after being away for several years, we lived in a different house farther from the store. Even so, I often visited it with my Aunt Clara who, in the absence of children of her own, always took a strong interest in me. Aunt Clara and Uncle D., mill workers, lived in a house across from ours in the village. Later, after permanently leaving the village, I continued to trade at the store into my teenage years. In the process of these visits, I came to know several people who clerked there.

Among the clerks was Ruby Dunn. Ruby was then a young woman who was married to Henry Dunn, an assistant superintendent in the Bladenboro Cotton Mills. The Dunns lived for a while in one of the better company houses (the rumor was that it had indoor plumbing) behind the store on a street that ran perpendicular to that on which our family lived. Later the Dunns (perhaps to separate themselves from the negative reputation of the cotton mill culture) built a substantial home on Front Street, where they spent the rest of their lives among the mill-owning families. I well remember Ruby because she clerked in the most important part of the store for a child—where the soda fountain, the candy showcase, and the ice cream were located. I remember her also because of her kindness to me. She was always pleasant, always made a fuss about my long eyelashes and my hair, always acted in a way that was pleasing to a child like me. Because she was a smiling, cheerful, kindly woman, I am certain that her treatment of me was no exception. She related to all the mill children whom she met in the store in the same friendly way. And the workers too! I recall that mill hands standing at the fountain in their overalls—most of whom Ruby easily addressed by their first names—received the same courteous treatment. She treated everyone with courtesy and respect, characteristics that she retained throughout the rest of her long life.

Another memorable person was Emmett Guyton, who managed the company store. As noted above, he was conspicuous because his manner of dress indicated that he was someone important. He always wore a white shirt and tie that set him apart from the other male clerks, who rarely wore such clothing. I came to know Mr. Emmett very well because of the arrangement that my father had made with him and Mrs. Maggie about letting me have items from the store, which were then charged to my father's account. As I remember, Emmett was a tall man who wore glasses and had a high-pitched voice. Three episodes stand out concerning him.

Once, when I was about four, I went to the store to purchase a quart of milk, which was then sold in glass containers. On leaving the store, I dropped the container, smashing the glass and spilling the milk in the doorway. It was an awful mess! Emmett had the mess quickly cleared away and the milk replaced, all the while calming down a very frightened little boy.

On another errand to the store, without permission I purchased a beautiful harmonica on display in the front showcase. Although it cost twenty-five cents, then nearly three hours' wages, Emmett did not hesitate to let me have it because of his arrangement with my father. However, my mother insisted that I return it. After sitting on the back porch and blowing the instrument for a while, I returned it to the store, and Emmett reluctantly accepted it.

I remember his being upset with me only once. As a second grader, I stopped by the store to purchase food for a school lunch (children took their lunches to school then because the Bladenboro Public Schools did not have a school lunch program until the mid-forties) before catching the village school bus. I selected and pointed to a candy bar in the showcase. Because he was busy talking to another customer, Emmett handed me the wrong candy bar. When I told him about his error, he said in an exasperated voice, "I swear, boy, you said you wanted the candy I gave you." However, he exchanged the candy and renewed his conversation with his customer.

I continued an off-and-on contact with Emmett until his death. After the death of his wife and older daughter, Thelma, years after his work in the store, he was forced into a nursing home in nearby Elizabethtown because of serious illness. My father and I visited him there. He had become a pitiable figure, a victim of diabetes, which necessitated amputations and created other health problems. A lonely and broken man, Emmett died shortly after our last visit.

Although Mrs. Margaret Bridger was not part of the clerking staff at the company store, she nevertheless made a lasting impression on me. Like Ruby Dunn, she was a kindly lady who treated everyone with courtesy and respect. Working with Miller Bridger in the office near the backdoor entrance to the store, she was in a position from her perch to observe nearly everything that went on in the store. Her job as dispenser of credit in the form of the company's Maggie's gold put her into contact with nearly every worker in the Bladenboro Cotton Mills, most of whom she knew and called by their first names. She was a small, fragile woman who wore glasses. For some reason (possibly because she admired the way my father placed so much trust in me as a very young boy), Mrs. Maggie took a liking to me. And I liked her. It was a friendship that lasted throughout the rest of her life, even though I saw her only infrequently after leaving the area for college.

On Fridays the company store always made fish available to its customers. With freshwater fish caught from the various rivers and ponds around Bladenboro, the weekly meals of mill families frequently included a "mess" of fish. Eating fish—fresh or canned—once or twice a week was very common. For instance, regular dishes in our family were stewed canned salmon and rice, salmon patties and rice, and fried fish and rice. These meals were always—winter or summer—accompanied by tall glasses of sweetened iced tea and either hot biscuits or cornmeal fritters.

The company store exploited this ready market for a food product that was easily attainable from coastal wholesalers. During the early morning hours of Friday, a truck loaded with saltwater fish dropped off several boxes the size of orange crates behind the store. The boxes were filled with undressed spot, mullet, croaker, flounder, and bream, all packed in ice to preserve them. Knowing that Friday was "fish" day at the store, some customers arrived early, as soon as the store opened, in order to have the first choice of fish. Customers stood around the crates, picking up the fish and carefully examining them for freshness. A clerk weighed, wrapped, and tied their purchase in old newspapers.

Even after our family had moved from the Old Mill village, my mother often sent me to the company store early on Friday morning to purchase fish, usually two, admonishing me that I should inspect them carefully because if they were not fresh, she would send them back. Of course, she gave me lessons in what to look for to determine their freshness. Occasionally my selection failed to satisfy her, and at her insistence I reluctantly returned them, rewrapped in the same old newspaper, and asked again for fish that were fresh. The spot was her favorite; my father preferred the mullet because of its somewhat bitter taste. However, the fish that I purchased usually depended on what the wholesaler had left that morning. Selling at two pounds for a quarter, fish were a cheap, wholesome element in the worker's diet. After eating saltwater and canned fish throughout the winter, many mill families looked forward to the warm sunny days of spring because they longed for a "mess" of freshwater fish, which tasted different from fish from the sea.

Workers traded at the store of the Bladenboro Cotton Mills for various reasons. Perhaps the most important was the availability of credit there during the hard times of the Great Depression. With the mills running on short-time (fewer shifts because of limited orders), there was little ready cash available among workers for trade outside the villages in the few mercantile establishments in nearby Bladenboro. The absence of cash left them without the option to buy elsewhere. With the creation of the fiat money system by the company, workers could draw Maggie's gold at the store office on their unpaid wages for use in the store. Or, if they had not accumulated any backlog of unpaid wages because there was no work, they might request the coins at the office as a form of credit against their future wages. Such loans were deducted from their pay envelopes on the next payday. Like the Bridger Corporation Store and other stores in the area that "carried" farmers until their crops were harvested in the fall, the company store undoubtedly imposed interest charges on workers who borrowed against future wages. However, with no other source of income or help, workers with a reputation for honesty and hard work found the store a refuge when confronted with little or no work.

Many workers—even those with the means to trade elsewhere—patronized the company store because of convenience. Very few of them had automobiles, and there was no public transportation from the villages into town. Unlike the stores in Bladenboro, which were located nearly a mile away, the company store was adjacent to the villages and within easy walking distance. To carry heavy bags of groceries from it to home was much easier than from the town stores. (During the thirties stores in Bladenboro did not deliver customers' purchases as they were later to do briefly after the war.) When village residents without transportation quickly needed specific items (a gallon of milk or meat for a meal), they went to the company store, where these items were readily and conveniently available.

However, with the closing of the store and the mills at noon on Saturday, there was a migration out of the villages along Highway 211 into town, where mill families, if they had the means, purchased items not found in the company store, got their hair cut, attended a matinee at W. G. Fussell's Lyric Theater, or spent hours standing on the street talking, smoking, and chewing tobacco. For village residents, as for their agricultural counterparts in the region, a visit to Bladenboro on Friday afternoon or Saturday was a "must." In most instances, "going to town" was more for social than commercial reasons. It provided an opportunity to renew contacts with friends and family members whom they had not seen for awhile.

As a historical institution, the company store does not have a good reputation. In most historical literature, it generally has been portrayed as an exploiter and gouger of workingmen for the benefit of their employers. If the company store of the Bladenboro Cotton Mills was such an institution, most workers seemed unaware that it was so. Over the years I never heard my father or relatives who worked in the mills state that the store was exploitive. They never complained in my presence that the price of its merchandise was higher than that found in town stores. Nor did they ever complain that they were required or "forced" to trade at the company store, although circumstances may have made trade there their only choice. Nor did they ever complain that the company clerks, some of whom they had known since childhood, treated them in a disrespectful or condescending manner. On the contrary, from my observations the relationship between the clerks and the workers was cordial and friendly. My father was on a first-name basis with all the clerks, including the manager, Emmett Guyton.

Of course, my father was an honest, responsible man who was admired for those traits. It is possible that individual workers without those characteristics did not merit the same respect and consideration that he received from store personnel. For instance, he recalls overhearing a dispute about debt and credit between a very angry worker and a calm Miller Bridger at the store's office window. In the exchange, the upset worker directed profane and abusive language toward Bridger who, he charged, was deliberately and wrongly refusing him the credit he deserved. He was so angry that he was incapable of understanding Miller's patient explanation that he was already much overextended. This worker left the store convinced that he had been unfairly treated by the company. With deductions for the doctor, the store, the rent, and hospital insurance being taken from a worker's pay envelope to the extent that sometimes little money was left, it is not surprising that a refusal of credit at the company store, which represented the only source of necessities for some, generated such anger and hostility. With practically no alternative employment available because of the Great Depression, and with few sources of charitable assistance available, even an honest and responsible worker with a family, blindsided by illness or lack of work, could feel frustrated and angry if denied additional credit at the company store.

At times, the ability to obtain credit at the company store led some workers to create debt from which it was difficult to extricate themselves. The practice of the Bladenboro Cotton Mills of allowing pre-payday loans to its workers only in Maggie's gold indirectly imposed a hardship on employees who were desperately strapped for cash to purchase items not found in the company store. The obvious intent of the company was to encourage its workers to use its store. In doing so, the company made life substantially more difficult for its workers, who deserved better, and it cast a blot on the character of the store that served them.

The company store of the Bladenboro Cotton Mills that thrived during the thirties and forties no longer exists because of extraordinary changes that occurred in the textile industry in the post–World War II era. A crucial factor it its demise was the company's decision—perhaps as an economy measure such as other textile companies embraced at the time—to rid itself of the two villages, which housed hundreds of people. Scores of houses were given to residents—with the stipulation that they move them off company property to another site. A number of workers accepted this offer. The responsibility for the disposal of the houses fell to Charles Hasbrook, a longtime official of the company. (Because of our family's earlier connection with the mills, my mother requested and received one of the houses from Hasbrook but, unfortunately, an arsonist torched the building before she could ever claim possession.) Several entrepreneurs gained possession of a number of the houses, moved them across town, renovated them, and then rented them out as government-subsidized housing—occasionally to former mill workers who had lived in them. As a result, some of the houses from the villages, many of which had been built by lumber supplied by my grandfather Charley Edwards, continue to survive. With the removal of the village residents, the customer base of the company store was gone, and there was no longer a need for a company store. Later, the Bridger family sold out its interests in the mills, and the new owners converted the old store building to other uses.

If one enters Bladenboro from the west along Highway 211 past the mills on the left, one will not see the building that was once the company store. It is now structurally incorporated into what was the Old Mill, with little evidence of its former existence. Like the two villages, which have now been replaced with government-subsidized brick duplexes, the company store of the Bladenboro Cotton Mills is gone. The institution that touched the lives of so many workers and their families has faded into history.

Chapter 14

LEISURE TIME AND
THE MILL HANDS

DURING THE HARD times of the Great Depression, workers in the Bladenboro Cotton Mills often had time on their hands, especially when the mills were running part-time or not at all because of a lack of orders for yarn. Furthermore, the owners' method of scheduling work in the crisis added to this free time. To be "fair" and to retain a viable workforce when orders were few or nonexistent, the owners, rather than throw scores of workers into total unemployment, elected to distribute the available work so that the families of their employees—some of them large—who lived in the Old and New Mill villages were not made destitute. Access to a minimal income enabled the workers to pay, at least partially, their rent for company housing, their obligations at the company store, and the doctors who treated them.

Thus the practice of parceling out work was not only fair but humane. For in the absence of nonmill jobs during an era of high unemployment among all the nation's industrial workers, the company's employees dwelling in the two villages (the bulk of the workforce) were totally dependent on the meager wages they earned in the mills. This dependency remained even after the ameliorating New Deal measures of Franklin D. Roosevelt had been initiated following his election in 1932. My father recalls that during the thirties, especially the early years when the Depression reached its lowest point in terms of unemployment, he occasionally ran a set of frames only three eleven-hour shifts a week (sometimes less) and received nine cents an hour for his work. Although paid little for his labor during this shortened work week, he nonetheless considered himself fortunate to have *any* work because jobs were so difficult to find.

More leisure time occurred because the owners ran the mills only half the day on Saturdays, shutting down for the weekend at two o'clock, when the first shift ended. And, of course, until World War II created a heavy demand for yarn, Sunday was not a workday because the region's strong religious tradition dictated that the Sabbath was a day of rest ordained by God and Scripture.

As a boy who lived in several company houses in the Old Mill village and in a house near the village during my teenage years, I was able to observe and listen to stories about how the mill people used the leisure time that was often imposed on them for pleasure and necessities. Among the men a favorite pastime was fishing, an activity that was cheap and inexpensive. A number of rivers, swamps, ponds, and lakes were located within easy driving or walking distance of the Bladenboro Cotton Mills. These waters included the Cape Fear River, the South River, Black River, the Big Swamp, the Singletary, White, Bridger, Nance, Suggs (no relation to author), Bryant and other millponds, and the half-dozen state-owned lakes of Bladen County. Although the lakes were as easily accessible as many of the streams and ponds, I don't recall ever knowing or hearing of mill workers who fished these publicly owned waters such as Black or Singletary Lake—for fishing these large lakes required not only a license but expensive equipment like a boat, which had to be transported by a vehicle of some kind. Most workers neither had nor could afford such things. Nor did I ever know any worker who fished the Cape Fear River near Elizabethtown, which included commercial fish like shad below the locks, fish that were not found in the other waters nearby. Like the public lakes, the Cape Fear, the largest of the streams in the immediate vicinity, required greater effort and more equipment than was required to fish, for example, the Big Swamp.

Nor did mill employees often fish the nearby millponds, which were privately owned. For example, Bridger's Millpond was owned by Dr. Dewey H. Bridger, and Nance's Millpond was owned by Fred Nance, a local farmer and mail carrier. Such waters were generally closed to all but families and friends. Consequently, to pond fish one had to receive special permission from an owner, a privilege that most of them were reluctant to grant to the socially distant mill people. Of the nearby millponds, Singletary's Pond, located several miles north of Bladenboro off Highway 131, was the one most frequently fished by mill workers because of the tolerance of its owner, June Singletary, a local farmer active in the educational and political affairs of the Bladen County. From time to time, my father and his brothers Noah and Major fished for bream, perch, jack, and other fish in Singletary's Pond and the creek that fed the catch basin located below the remains of an old grist mill that weathered away upon the milldam. And a few fellow workers from the mill villages did the same.

Nevertheless, pond fishing did not engage nearly as many mill people as townspeople. For many years during the summers of the thirties, nearly all the stores in Bladenboro closed at noon on Wednesdays, releasing their clerks for an afternoon of leisure, which, in the absence of other forms of recreation, usually meant fishing. This practice of Wednesday closing was to compensate the clerks for the late hours they worked on Fridays and Saturdays, when the town was flooded with people from the mill villages and the surrounding farms. Often the male clerks hurried off to fish the nearby ponds—whose owners, probably because they knew the clerks socially or from contacts in the stores or their churches, graciously granted them permission to do so.

Unable to gain access to the privately owned ponds, most mill employees frequented fishing sites along the South and Black Rivers, which formed the northeastern boundary of the county, and the Big Swamp, which formed the western boundary of the county. The Big Swamp, the nearest of the three streams, could be entered from many close-by points—Tar Keel Point, Lennons' Crossroads Bridge, Butters, and the Big Swamp bridge west on Highway 211. When workers were not in the mills, fishing these streams was an important activity for them. For in the hard times of the thirties, they fished not only for pleasure but for needed food. Once I heard a relative remark that workers at the Bladenboro Cotton Mills survived the Great Depression because of the abundance of cheap cornmeal, black strap molasses, and fish, especially catfish, from the Big Swamp.

I know about how frequently a few of the workers fished because they often hired me to dig the earthworms that they used for bait. The pay reflected the times—ten cents for a no. 2 tomato can full of worms. To fill such a can with choice black earthworms required great effort, an effort that became even greater as the thirties passed into the war years of the forties. The favorite digging site for me and others was in that portion of Bryant Swamp boxed in by the Seaboard Railway line, the Bridger fields, the Bladenboro Cotton Mills, and the town of Bladenboro. It was not uncommon for several teenagers to be digging bait in close proximity to each other. For here the worms once thrived underneath the cypress and black gums where the earth was cool, rich, and black. As the years passed, however, they became increasingly difficult to find because of the extensive digging that had occurred. More and more, one then found it necessary to rework ground that had already been exploited, where the earthworm population had been reduced to near extinction. Although there were other areas in Bryant Swamp where bait could be found, the depletion of this accessible site was a measure of the importance that fishing played in the leisure time of mill workers.

As a teenager, I not only dug bait for various mill workers but I also fished with them at the Big Swamp and the South River. Even with only simple equipment, some of the men were superb fishermen. Among the very best that I observed were Leslie Thompson and Willie Bowen, each of whom seemed to have a sixth sense for locating fish in a stream. Their equipment was the most elementary kind—a bamboo pole, black silk line, sinkers, and hooks. On occasion I had supplied Thompson with worms and therefore knew something about his excellent reputation as a fisherman. Once at South River I saw how really good he was. While walking the bank of the river looking for a place to fish, I came across Thompson as he fished around numerous roots in fast, turbulent water. At that point the stream was so shallow and swift that I would never have considered it a likely place to catch fish. It appeared to be only a perfect place for hanging hooks. But as I watched, Thompson methodically pulled one beautiful redbreast after another from the rooted spot, using as bait luscious black earthworms like the ones that I had supplied. As I watched him, I realized that I was watching an extraordinary performance. I forgot to fish. From my vantage point on the bank, I could see that others in Thompson's group were catching nothing as they watched his action from downstream, and the same was true for fishermen on the Sampson County side of the river. A rather large man, Thompson displayed great pleasure in the attention his prowess provoked, holding up each catch like a trophy for all of us to see.

Willie Bowen was another mill worker who was an excellent fisherman. Bowen was a member of the White Oak Original Free Will Baptist Church, and his daughters attended school with me, so I knew him much better than I did Leslie Thompson. Once when I was a teenager, my uncle invited me to go fishing with a group that included Bowen and two uncles (who worked in the mills) to the South River, where I observed firsthand Bowen's fishing skills. We left Bladenboro around four in the morning in order to be at the river shortly after sunrise. Like Leslie Thompson, Bowen seemed to have an instinct for finding fish in unexpected places in a stream. I watched him climb down a steep, brush-covered bank to fish a bend of the river that my uncles had bypassed because of the difficult access and because exposed roots and tree limbs were likely to entangle tackle. Bowen, a short, portly man, positioned himself precariously near the water and swung his hook and sinker into certain entanglement—and yet without a hitch proceeded to catch fifteen or twenty large redbreasts and other fish. Somehow he managed to avoid falling into the river while he pulled in the fish, secured his catch on a string, rebaited his hook, and tossed out his gear again and again. As I watched this master fisherman at work, I marveled not only at the fish he caught but at his ability to avoid losing tackle in the swirling water around the roots and limbs. Much to my surprise, he also exhibited great dexterity in moving his large frame about in a very limited space between the bank and the river. Although the two uncles caught fish that day, neither of them came close to matching the number on Bowen's string.

My father also loved to fish. During the early thirties, my father, my uncle, and friends such as Jetter Hester often fished the Big Swamp—and not always solely for pleasure. Like other fellow workers, they fished to supplement the family food supply. At the time, the Big Swamp, which separates Bladen County from Robeson County, was a slow-moving stream of clean black water that had an abundance of fish, and a "mess" of freshwater fish was a welcome addition to the foods obtainable at the company store. It was not uncommon for some mill workers on their days off to spend a day and perhaps a dangerous night together in the swamp fishing for the delicious black-skinned channel catfish by setting hooks along the bank of the stream. My father has vivid memories of several such anxious nights when, with flashlight in hand, he checked his hooks to the accompaniment of the screams of nearby wildcats while fighting to overcome a gripping fear of the large cottonmouth moccasins that inhabited the swamp and slithered about in the dark.

At times workers make a great effort to fish. I recall that my father once took me and my younger brother Charles on a fishing trip to the Big Swamp. To get there, we walked nearly four miles west along Highway 211. Upon arrival, we crossed the highway bridge and entered the swamp on the Robeson County side, where we had decided to fish a sluice that lay parallel to the highway and emptied into the mainstream. The sluice was shallow, filled with accumulated debris, and covered with overhanging branches. It looked impossible to fish and appeared to be a perfect habitat for water moccasins. But my father insisted that we try our luck along the bank of this unlikely fishing spot. Working his tackle carefully to avoid entangling it in the brush and foliage, my father began to catch blackfish, one after another, until he had a string of fifteen or more fish. He was a skillful fisherman. His luck ended, however, when my brother carelessly pulled a hook through his finger, forcing us to leave the swamp and seek a doctor. Fortunately, someone with a pickup truck was kind enough to stop and give us a lift into Bladenboro, where Dr. Dewey H. Bridger easily removed the hook by cutting off its barbed end. Our experience in walking to the Big Swamp was not uncommon for mill workers without transportation (very few had cars) and a desire to fish. They did not hesitate to walk either Highway 211 or the tracks of the Seaboard Railway to this popular fishing site.

Like their working fathers, many male youngsters also enjoyed fishing. After the creation of the Works Progress Administration (WPA), Bryant Swamp, which often flooded and wreaked havoc on homes and businesses around Bladenboro, was partially ditched by WPA laborers to accelerate the runoff of high water from the settled areas. Afterward, however, even in the absence of flood water, the normal flow through the drainage ditches was sufficient to encourage the proliferation of small catfish, about three to six inches long, that were a delight for youngsters to catch. Although not big enough to eat, these fish nevertheless permitted boys to hone their fishing skills for the occasional trips with parents to bigger streams such as the Big Swamp or the South River.

Beyond the system of ditches around the town, the waters of Bryant Swamp flowed in a more leisurely fashion to join the Big Swamp, spreading out branchlike to form shallow Simpson Lake, which was located nearly a quarter of a mile south of the Will Davis farm. Simpson Lake was not really a lake but a small collection basin that flooded the trunks of the cypress and blackgum trees growing there. It retained water year round. Simpson Lake contained many small panfish that were fun to catch. During the summers, boys from the mill villages often visited the lake to fish its waters, standing on stumps or fallen logs to do so. Although a few of the fish caught there were big enough to eat, few people ate them because that part of Bryant Swamp received the runoff from the collection pond of the Bladenboro Cotton Mills—into which flowed the sewerage generated by hundreds of workers in the mills.

Even so, this millpond, which lay between the Old and New Mills and extended out under the Highway 211 bridge to separate the Old Mill and the Seaboard Railway tracks, was also fished by youngsters living in the villages, as was the tea-colored branch that flowed into it. This branch had its origins in the swampy, lowland areas to the north of the cotton mills and separated the two mill villages. A tenuous foot-log crossed this wide shallow stream and linked the separated villages. Two bridges—one on Highway 211, the other a wooden company bridge—crossed the pond and connected the Old and New Mills. During the summer, barefooted boys from the villages fished the pond while standing on the wooden bridge that the company had built for foot traffic and other milling purposes. However, it was not uncommon for them to fish from the lower window of the cotton house, where a youngster like myself could drop tackle into the water several feet below. Workers in the cotton house were very tolerant of boys who fished there. Although the pond was heavily polluted—so much so that the flesh of its fish was colored a sickening yellow— it contained some large catfish that boys occasionally caught and showed excitedly to everyone.

Mill operatives were not the only ones connected with the Bladenboro Cotton Mills who enjoyed fishing in their leisure time. The owners and supervisors also actively engaged in the sport. Members of the Bridger clan who owned the mills regularly visited the Bridger Millpond, where a clubhouse had been built by Dr. Dewey H. Bridger for the use of the family. Located in a beautiful setting of pines and Bridger-owned farmland several miles from Bladenboro, the pond was kept well stocked with perch, brim, and bass. Family members and invited guests often used the clubhouse, which was equipped with a kitchen and a spacious dining room, for a fish fry and relaxing after an outing of fishing. On occasion, Dr. Bridger graciously permitted Boy Scout Troop 72, which included several sons of mill workers, to use his pond and clubhouse for scouting purposes during the mid-forties. Under the leadership of the Reverend Benjamin Ormand, a Presbyterian minister, members of the troop enjoyed fishing, frog gigging, and boating on the pond and camping under the pines.

In addition to Bridger Millpond, adult members of the Bridger clan enjoyed fishing from a privately owned site on the Black

River, where Joe Bridger had built a clubhouse, maintained by a caretaker. On weekends during the summer, adult members of the family frequented the isolated site for a day or two of fishing and relaxed living away from the prying eyes of the community. Once a member of the clan invited Graham Wilson, who headed the dry goods department of the Bridger Corporation Store in Bladenboro, to join a group of Bridgers for an overnight stay and a day of fishing at the Black River site. An excellent fisherman, Wilson was also a devout, straitlaced Free Will Baptist who refrained from using profanity, tobacco, or alcohol. When he returned, he described his fishing excursion to my father (who, like Wilson, was a Free Will Baptist) as one he would never forget. He reported that when morning came, his hosts left the clubhouse with the caretaker and embarked up the river in boats. Late that afternoon near sundown, he heard them returning, their loud yelling and singing reverberating up and down the river. According to Wilson, they climbed awkwardly from the boats, their fish boxes full, and their drenched caretaker in his underclothes. After they had left the boats, the caretaker—still partially clad and a wee bit tipsy—proceeded to clean the fish before frying them for the evening meal, a meal that Wilson avoided because of the unsavory appearance of the cook. The sport of fishing local waters provided the owners of the Bladenboro Cotton Mills with an opportunity to relax and let off steam, just as it did the scores of operatives working for them.

Owning summer cottages at Wrightsville, Carolina, Sunset, Ocean Drive, and perhaps other beaches on the Carolina coast, the mill owners also enjoyed fishing in coastal waters that were located approximately sixty to seventy miles from Bladenboro. To ordinary workers in their mills during the thirties, however, these beaches seemed to be at the other end of the earth, too far away and too expensive to visit. This was not true of the mill owners, whose families enjoyed an extended summer stay at the beach cottage, usually accompanied by a maid to cook and care for the children. For such families, lazy days of relaxing at the beach was a way of life, with husbands and fathers joining them on the weekends.

In a section of the cotton houses that lay parallel to the New Mill, Joe Bridger assigned mill carpenters, under the direction of Archie Pait, a master carpenter, the task of constructing a large, seaworthy cabin cruiser for boating and deep-sea fishing. Youngsters living in the villages, who had never seen such a large boat (nor, indeed, the ocean), watched its building with gawking interest because the vessel under construction was too large for the rivers, streams, and the accessible lakes in the area that were known to them. Occasionally, after delivering a meal to my father at work in the New Mill, I stopped in the shop to admire the skill of the carpenters as they labored on the boat. I was able to do so because Pait, who with his wife, Mary, were longtime members of my parents' church, knew me and tolerated my standing about in the workplace observing his crew. Upon its completion, Bridger removed his cruiser to some site on the coast. But for the rank-and-file workers in the mills, it was not until after World War II, when many world-traveled veterans returned to their jobs, that they began to discover and enjoy the delights of pier and surf fishing in the coastal waters of North and South Carolina, especially when the spots, whiting, and other fish were plentiful and running in the fall of the year.

Although fishing ranked near the top as the leisure activity most engaged in among workers in the Bladenboro Cotton Mills during the thirties and early forties, talking and storytelling were very close competitors. The textile workers I knew loved to talk and socialize. However, this love of conversation and storytelling was not unique to the people who composed the mill community. In the absence of radios, which many could not afford, television sets, which were not available, and the numerous other distractions of today, most of the people living in the Bladenboro area generally found ample time to engage in conversation with their neighbors, friends, and coworkers. Nevertheless, living in such close proximity in the villages, mingling and mixing in a confined workplace, frequently attending the same denominational churches, experiencing and sharing common, hard-time experiences of the Depression, sharing many family connections through marriages—all provided mill hands with numerous opportunities to know, talk, laugh, joke, quarrel, and cry with each other over matters directly affecting their lives. I recall numerous occasions when as a boy I sat and listened for hours as they talked and argued passionately about politics, religion, village events, fights, murders, women, sex, fishing, shutdowns, firings, scandals, baseball, the hard times, and other subjects.

In the spring, summer, and fall when the weather permitted, a favorite time for male workers to chitchat, smoke, and chew tobacco was shortly before the afternoon shift change, that half-hour period between the single, shift-announcing blast of the mill's steam whistle at one-thirty—a piercing, high-pitched whine that overrode the loud din of the mills throughout and beyond the villages—and, thirty minutes later, two similar blasts at two o'clock that marked the actual start of the day's second shift. It was not unusual for men scheduled for the second shift to leave home early in order to join one of the ever-changing groups that gathered principally at two sites outside the Old and New Mills.

At the Old Mill, the favored meeting place was in the shade of two large chinaberry trees located adjacent to Bill Hester's house across from the loading dock and railroad siding at the northeast end of the mill. Because of its close proximity to the mill, the din of the machines at the site sometimes made conversation difficult. However, men accustomed to communicating with each other around the machines while at work did not seem to find the lesser outside noise a bother. Early arrivals positioned themselves under the trees, either sitting atop discarded cola crates or squatting on the balls of their feet, all the while smoking cigarettes, chewing tobacco, whittling or, perhaps, drinking from bottles of Coca-Cola or Pepsi-Cola. As the shift change approached, their numbers rapidly increased. Newcomers en route to work paused and stood on the periphery of the crowd, listening but rarely participating in the discussions, ready to dash into the mill at the last moment. But even after the whistle had signaled the start of the shift, a few malingerers stayed a while to speak to friends who were leaving the Old Mill after working the first shift.

Meanwhile, workers arriving at the New Mill for the second shift gathered in the shade of the raised platform that connected the mill's picker room with the nearby cotton houses that paralleled the mill. Before entering the workplace, amid the din they talked, smoked, and chewed the minutes away in lively conversation and argument. Like the group at the Old Mill, that at the New was ever-changing, as workers drifted in and out, staying if the subject interested them or quickly moving on if it did not. At times, when a subject like baseball or politics was being argued, their numbers swelled, filling the cramped space under the platform and causing subgroups to form. As the hour of two o'clock approached, a few workers on the first shift began trickling from the mill as their workday ended, sometimes stopping on the fringe to listen or participate in whatever subject was under discussion. But when the last whistle blew there was a flood of movement, just as at the Old Mill, with workers on the first shift pouring en masse from the mill entrance as their less enthusiastic replacements for the next shift entered to operate the machines. Within a few minutes after the final whistle, except for a shirker or two the meeting places under the chinaberry trees at the Old Mill and the platform at the New Mill were silent and empty of workers.

On lazy Sunday afternoons in the spring, summer, and fall, when the mills did not run, workers had plenty of time for talking after attending church (and many did!) and eating "dinner." Then, with nothing to do, numbers of them met at a favorite meeting place at the end of the Old Mill, the end opposite the company store; there, depending on the weather, talking, whittling, chewing, and smoking were carried on for hours. Unhurried by whistles, shift changes, or demands of the job, mill hands whiled away the afternoon, regaling each other with local news and tall tales. Sitting with backs against the end of the mill or squatting on the balls of their feet, most members of the group listened as one or two recognized storytellers spun their fantastic yarns about eccentric individuals or relatives, psychic experiences with ghosts, recent religious revivals in which so-and-so "got saved," "Holy Roller" preachers, the latest gossip about marital breakups, lecherous bosses, promiscuous women, people in trouble with the law, sources of the best bootleg or "stump-hole" whiskey, and recent shootings and knifings in the villages. The membership of the group constantly changed, people coming and going as the afternoon slipped away. Each newcomer contributed his two cents' worth, enriching the conversation with a new angle or a new interpretation of the story under way, and each departing person carried away a head full of gossip and stories to spread next day in the workplace. For many workers, there was no better way to spend a Sunday afternoon than laughing and talking at the end of the Old Mill.

Among the better storytellers was Bud Edwards, who enthralled his listeners. Bud was one of the several sons of Latt Edwards, who owned the farmland adjacent to and east of the Old Mill village. Both Bud and his brother, Sam, worked in the Old Mill, while another brother, Airy, worked for the Seaboard railroad. After the death of their parents, the brothers rented out their inherited farm to supplement their income. Bud was a superb natural storyteller who was fully aware of his power to hold the attention of fellow workers who gathered at the end of the Old Mill on Sunday afternoons. He had the capacity to take a mundane incident in the lives of the workers and embellish it into a humorous, captivating story. Because of his skill, Bud usually dominated the conversation of the men who sat around smoking, chewing, dipping, and whittling. As the cigarette butts, tobacco juice, and wood shavings accumulated on the ground, Bud, munching on a bit of tobacco, told one story after another, sometimes repeating himself as the afternoon wore on. Nobody seemed to mind the repetition, however, because, like all good storytellers, he constantly added a new element to an old tale that made it seem new. At times, the life of the group greatly depended on Bud and the time he had to spend. For usually when he left, the members gradually dispersed, going their separate ways, unless, of course, another storyteller appeared on the scene to keep the chatter going—which was often the case. In the late forties, Bud left the mill, where his wife continued to work, to set up a small business on the edge of the Old Mill village. Thereafter, many of his former fellow workers gathered on Sunday afternoons under the towering pines near Bud's store and talked the hours away. As a teenager, I sometimes listened in on these talk sessions under the pines, squatting on the balls of my feet like the rest of the men or leaning against one of the pines.

Not all workers convened at the end of the Old Mill for conversation. The front porch was then an essential part of nearly every house, and the porch provided a favorite meeting place for endless conversations, especially for family members working in the mills. On sunny nonwork days in the villages, they often sat on porches or steps and talked to whomever passed by. And the same was true for mill families who lived outside the villages. For example, on Sunday afternoons, members of the Daniel Hester family usually met on Leland Shipman's front porch, where conversations might extend well into the evening. Shipman's house was located on Highway 211 about a quarter of a mile east of the mills. After Daniel's death, his widow, Exie, moved into the home of her daughter Rachel, Shipman's wife.

The Hesters were my mother's people. The family was large, consisting of five sons and three living daughters, all uncles and aunts of my mother. With the exception of one daughter, Tyne, who lived in St. Pauls, and one son, Blaine, all of them and most of their adult children worked in the Bladenboro Cotton Mills during the late thirties and early forties. Because Exie, the widowed mother of the clan and also my great-grandmother, lived with the Shipmans, the front porch of their home became the meeting place for family members. With cane in hand, an old, enfeebled Exie sat in a rocker on the porch as her children—George, Blaine, Bob, Seth, Jim, Rachel, Maryanne—and numerous grandchildren dropped by to "sit a spell." There was a constant coming and going of family members who, like most of their fellow workers in the mills, freely used cigarettes, chewing tobacco, and snuff. Throughout the afternoon the Hesters, occasionally joined by others walking alongside Highway 211, discussed a range of subjects, although their conversation tended to focus on the events occurring at the nearby White Oak Original Free Will Baptist Church, which the family dominated; work in the mills, where Bob and George were shift bosses; or family matters. Rocking, fanning, spitting, and smoking, they sat and talked for hours at a time, interrupted only by visits to the outhouse to answer nature's call, a trek to the overflow at the back of the house for a cool drink of water, or the appearance of newcomers. Toward evening, as darkness fell, hordes of mosquitoes emerged from nearby Bryant Swamp to harass the group, forcing Rachel to set out smoke pots full of smoldering rags to drive them away. However, if the conversation were lively (for example, concerning the outbreak of war in Europe or the possibility of the United States entering the conflict), not even the pestiferous, bloodsucking mosquitoes stopped the discussion. Members of the Hester clan were an opinionated group, with no reluctance whatsoever about revealing either their knowledge or ignorance on any subject that anyone on the porch cared to bring up. Their talk was therefore frequently marked by outbreaks of friendly arguments and boisterous disagreements that were promptly forgotten as the conversation flowed on to another subject. As a member of the family who lived a short distance from the Shipmans, I was often a silent participant in these fascinating Sunday-afternoon talkathons on the Shipmans' front porch.

My father's people, the Suggses, were also an argumentative, talkative group that met often on Sunday afternoon at their parents' home. Like Daniel and Exie Hester, Asie and Fannie Suggs, my paternal grandparents, raised a large family of five sons and three daughters—Arthur (Artie), Noah, John, Major, George, Clara, Mae, Kate—all of whom began working at an early age in either the Bladenboro Cotton Mills or other area textile mills located in East Lumberton, Hope Mills, St. Pauls, Wilmington, or Rockingham. With the exception of Artie and John, who left the mills for other occupations such as farming, the Suggses spent most of their working lives in the Bladenboro Cotton Mills, a few of them sometimes combining mill work with farming. And so did their spouses.

Before the family members began to disperse after the United States entered World War II, on Sunday afternoon the Suggses, just like the Hesters, usually gathered on the front porch of some family member's house, where they spent hours arguing and talking about current events, their jobs in the mills, the status of crops, politics, religion, family matters, and whatever came to mind. On occasions they met at Artie's farmhouse. Artie, the oldest of the children, had taken on the responsibility of caring for my aging grandparents. After a "dinner" prepared by Grandma Suggs and whatever daughter was present, everyone retired outside to sit in the shade of several trees, where they spent the afternoon talking. Like the Hesters—but in a more limited way—the Suggses used tobacco to facilitate conversation. The women in the family dipped snuff; Grandpa Suggs chewed from a plug of homemade tobacco and smoked Prince Albert tobacco from a homemade corncob pipe; Major, John, and Noah smoked cigarettes and occasionally cheap King Edward cigars. Only Artie entirely abstained from tobacco; my father, George, never smoked—except at these family meetings. Every conversation was punctuated by someone lighting up, leaning forward to spit into a vacant area, or reaching for a "spit can." Unlike the Hesters' meetings on the Shipmans' front porch, as evening approached on Artie's farm, the Suggs clan usually dispersed, using Major's and Noah's cars to return home.

What happened on the front porches of the Shipmans and the Suggses was duplicated throughout the Old and New Mill villages. Most residents engaged in porch-and-step talk, conversation occasionally interrupted and enlivened by a radio broadcast of a ball game—if the householder possessed a radio—or spontaneous entertainment of some kind. For example, Lambert Coleman, a consumptive-looking young man who worked in the Old Mill, was very skilled at playing the mandolin. Sometimes Coleman sat on his or someone else's front porch or steps and, with pick in hand, played tunes on the delicate instrument, creating music on a quiet Sunday afternoon that was heard by numerous others chatting on nearby porches. And, if neighbors gathered—as they invariably did—the group often broke out in a sing-along to Coleman's music, especially if it involved familiar country tunes heard on the Grand Ole Opry. Coleman had always dreamed of having his own band; after the war he formed a group that performed on a radio station out of Lumberton. He was sponsored by local advertisers like the Jack Pait Furniture Company, the Hussy Brothers Grocery, and other small businesses. Unfortunately, he never realized his ambition to go "big time" with his music. His most appreciative audience was the neighbors in the Old Mill village who gathered around to enjoy his playing.

Mill families found other ways to enjoy their leisure time. Small town that it was, Bladenboro had its Lyric Theater, which ran evening movies throughout the week—except, of course, on Sunday evening. Like other local businesses, the theater was closed on the Sabbath, which the community considered a day for rest and religious observance. For people in the villages, however, the Saturday showings, which usually consisted of a western film (starring men like Tom Mix, Buck Jones, Hopalong Cassidy, Roy Rogers, or Johnny Mack Brown), a serial, and a comedy, were the ones most frequently attended. W. G. Fussell, owner of the Lyric, encouraged their attendance by accepting Maggie's gold (at a discount) in payment for tickets. Like most Americans during the Great Depression of the thirties, unless restrained by religious conviction, workers in the Bladenboro Cotton Mills enjoyed the movies as an escape from the hard times.

With the coming of spring and summer, baseball always captured the interest of many workers to an extraordinary degree. Before World War II, the Spinners, the company's baseball team, drew scores of workers and their families out to see the games that were played on a diamond next to Bladenboro High School. Located more than a mile from the mills, the school diamond and its wooden grandstand were surrounded by a wooden fence, which repeatedly echoed the crack of bat on balls when spring practice began. During the baseball season, the Spinners played a schedule of games as a member of a textile league consisting of mill teams in the region, supported principally by family-owned cotton mills.

As I recall, these games were well attended because baseball was an obsession with many mill workers, who religiously followed the home team and their favorite teams in the national leagues. Consequently, when an opportunity came to watch their Spinners or the local high school team play, their enthusiasm for the game caused them to turn out in numbers. As noted elsewhere, the Bladenboro Cotton Mills underwrote the expenses of the Spinners, providing uniforms, equipment, transportation, and employing coaches and key players. After the war, the management of the mills constructed Spinners' Field adjacent to the New Mill village west of Bladenboro, making it easily accessible by foot for the residents of both villages. Playing, watching, and talking baseball were important leisure activities for mill workers. The game was the subject of frequent conversation in the barbershops, the workplace, and on numerous front porches.

In the late thirties Bladenboro had a small library, which had been created to honor Henry Clyde Bridger, a member of the mill-owning Bridger family, who had succumbed to tuberculosis. Bridger had been an avid reader; his collection of books, after proper fumigation, became the core of the library's limited holdings. Under the supervision of Miss Bertha Sandidge, an elderly, white-haired woman who zealously protected each book as if it were something very special, the library loaned books principally to town residents who lived within easy walking distance of the Women's Club building where it was situated.

Unlike the town, the Old and New Mill villages did not have a library. Although village residents were free to borrow books from the town facility because it was incorporated into the Bladen County library system, its distance from the mills precluded a heavy use by workers and their families—even had there been an inclination to do so. However, I don't think that there was such an inclination. In an age when the children of workers were expected to follow their parents into the mills, when, for that reason, many village parents perceived no value in having their children complete high school, and when books and education were thought of as extraneous luxuries that interfered with the hard job of earning an immediate living—in such an age, reading, studying, and reflecting were not top priorities. However, newspapers such as the *Charlotte Observer* and the *Grit* were delivered in both villages. For a very short while, I delivered the daily *Charlotte Observer* to some thirty customers there and the weekly *Grit* to about half a dozen, which showed that some workers read and kept abreast of current events. And, of course, many churchgoers dutifully read their Bibles and other denominational materials in preparation for Sunday services. As a whole, however, the textile workers whom I knew were not avid readers.

Yet in spite of the prevailing attitudes about the necessity and desirability of learning, some working parents and their children found great pleasure in reading, learning, and schooling. Myra Lou Stubbs, the teenage daughter of Joe Stubbs, a minor supervisor in the Old Mill, was a voracious reader who undoubtedly borrowed and read more books from the Henry Clyde Bridger Library than any town resident. The Stubbs, who had formerly lived in the Old Mill village, lived two doors down from our house on Highway 211. Myra Lou walked to the library and returned with her arms loaded with books. During the summer when school was not in session, she often sat on her front porch, several books by her chair, and read for hours at a time. For her, reading was an enjoyable way to spend her leisure time, but she was the only one in the Stubbs family to think so.

Unfortunately, I recall only a few other children of mill workers who took such an obvious delight in reading. One was Vernon Hester, whose parents lived in the Old Mill village and worked in the mills. Vernon was driven to complete high school; unknowingly, he inspired me and possibly others to do the same. Several years older than I, he arose before daybreak to deliver the *Charlotte Observer* before leaving for school. Later, after turning his paper route over to me, he attended high school in the morning and worked the second shift at the mill. He succeeded in completing high school, in those days a significant achievement for the children of mill workers. Using the G.I. Bill after serving in World War II, Vernon graduated from Duke University. He was the first person from the villages of the Bladenboro Cotton Mills to receive a degree from a major university. He was not the last. For after the war, which opened up a myriad of opportunities for all classes of people, children from the villages completed high school and college in growing numbers.

For many workers and their families, church activities consumed much of their leisure time, especially on Sunday when they attended both morning and evening services. The hard times of the thirties undoubtedly encouraged scores of them to turn to religion for solace and comfort. In the several churches around the villages, the membership consisted principally of mill people, who were conspicuous in leadership roles and all religious activities. As noted elsewhere, workers took their responsibilities in these bodies very seriously, some of them electing to combine an active ministry with their work in the mills.

However, as in any large group, there were many workers who had little use for religion or the church and found other, nonreligious ways to spend their leisure hours. Among these activities were gambling in all-night poker sessions in the nearby woods of Bryant Swamp, spending an entire Saturday shooting pool in Pelo Lockamy's pool hall, drinking themselves into a state of oblivion (or the local jail), or spending the day in town doing as little as possible. In the use of leisure time, workers made their own choices how that time would be spent.

Conclusion

CHANGING WORLDS

The cotton mill culture existing throughout the South in the first half of the twentieth century—my father's world, which he sadly concluded was "gone"—did not disappear overnight. To astute observers of his generation, signs of its demise were already evident as early as the start of the thirties. Foreign competition, the introduction of synthetic fabrics such as rayon, changing clothing styles, and new labor-displacing technologies were—even in my father's prime—already nibbling away at his world of mill villages, speeders, slubbers, intermediates, carding, winding, spinning, warping, and other machines.

Understandably, however, as a young mill hand during the twenties and thirties, he, like thousands of widely scattered cotton mill workers throughout the South, was not really aware when these subtle eroding developments began to undermine life as he then knew it. This blindness to the long-range impact that emerging market forces of that era would play on the textile industry was not limited solely to mill hands. Many owners and managers, especially in the southern states where cotton milling had flourished in the late nineteenth and early twentieth centuries, also failed to recognize the ultimate consequences that these economic changes would have on their industry. Even had owners, managers, and workers been fully aware of the long-range results, however, it is unlikely that they could have significantly altered the final outcome. For the cotton mill world of my father and his coworkers was destined to end bit by bit—industrial changes worked relentlessly to end it.

After I had written and reread several times the descriptive bits and pieces of life that characterized the world that my father had known as a young man in the Bladenboro Cotton Mills—

the loss of which he had so nostalgically lamented on our last visit to the former site of the Old Mill village—I remembered another of his worlds that was also gone, an earlier one that had repeatedly called to him during his years in the mills. He often expressed a strong desire to reenter that world and leave cotton milling behind. And he probably would have done so had the times and his family circumstances been different. What was that world? Farming!

Before entering the mills, my paternal grandparents had owned a small patch farm in Columbus County, North Carolina. Strong idealistic memories of life on the farm stayed with my father after he entered the mills. Often he reflected longingly on how quiet and peaceful life was in the country, how a man was free to come and go as he pleased, how a man could be his own boss, how clean and fresh the air was, and how he loved to watch crops growing in the fields. (At ninety-five he continued to "make" a garden.) His yearning to return to the land was strong, especially in springtime when the warm March winds of southeastern North Carolina caused buds to swell and leaves to burst out on plants and trees. Having a bachelor brother (Artie) who had left the mills to return to farming, another brother (John) who farmed, and another brother (Major) who combined farming with mill work only served to whet further his desire to do the same. At family gatherings when their conversation turned to crops, anticipated yields, weather, harvest, and prices, my father usually fell into a conspicuous silence—for he had nothing to contribute. At times during the thirties he seriously considered leaving the mills and purchasing farm property, which was then cheap because of the Depression. It was not to be. Times were too difficult; there was no money, not even for cheap land. Furthermore, my mother's illness precluded such a move because she was unable to do the heavy work required of most farm wives of that era, work that was necessary to assure economic success—indeed, survival. Consequently, although I am certain that he continued to dream of an idealized life on the farm, especially when conditions were difficult in the mills, he finally concluded that his dream of returning to the land could never be. However, the attitudes and perspectives about life and work that he acquired on the farm in Columbus County remained firmly entrenched as he entered the world of cotton milling to work for more than a quarter of a century. Had the nation not entered World War II in 1941, he undoubtedly would have remained a mill hand there for the rest of his working life.

The war produced an extraordinary industrial expansion. As the country converted to full wartime production, new opportunities for employment in factories and shipyards abounded. In the summer of 1942, when he was thirty-seven years old, my father left the Bladenboro Cotton Mills for the Wilmington shipyard, where he remained until early 1946. It was a new world of work that was exciting and full of danger, made more so by the daily commute of sixty miles from Bladenboro to Wilmington on an ancient school bus constantly in need of repair . Like many workers in the yard, he suffered injuries—mashed toes, a broken foot, and cracked ribs. Nevertheless, he enjoyed his years in the shipyard. His wages were higher from the start than those he had received in the cotton mills, and he relished being able to work outdoors. Further, he commuted to Wilmington with longtime friends, many of whom had also worked in the mills for years. The bonding that had resulted from their common mill experiences was made stronger by the comradery forged as much by their daily commute to the shipyard in an old school bus as by their common involvement in producing prefabricated Liberty ships.

When the war ended, the shipyard shut down. My father returned to the Bladenboro Cotton Mills, where he competed with much younger men—many of them returning veterans—for the available work. Now in his forties and with no other jobs available in Bladenboro, he gladly returned to running intermediate frames in the world he had left behind. He remained there until 1952, when he left the mills to follow an older brother, Noah, to Newport News, Virginia. There he worked for the Newport News Shipbuilding Company until he was laid off in 1955. Again he returned to the Bladenboro Cotton Mills to run frames, this time for a year. Recalled to work in Newport News in 1956, he remained there until severe injuries on the job forced his retirement in 1967. He never returned to work in the mills.

As my father grew older, I became increasingly aware how important the years in the cotton mills had been to him. Although while there he had often yearned to return to the land where he had spent part of his earliest boyhood, and although he had spent his last work years in the shipyards, it was the cotton mill world that seemed to dominate his thoughts and memories of the past. It wasn't that his memories of life on the farm and in the shipyards were not important to him, or that his life in the mills had obliterated all thoughts of those experiences from his mind. On the contrary, he liked to recall and discuss his memories of work in these places, memories that included his boyhood activities on the farm, friends and fellow workers in the shipyards, injustices and injuries suffered there, assessments of yard supervisors, and humorous episodes that occurred during the commute. However, it was memories of his life in the mills, particularly the Bladen-boro Cotton Mills, that ranked highest in his hierarchy of recall, memories that seemed to define who he truly was.

I often wondered why this was so. Perhaps the major reason was that his years in the mills coincided with his youth and the most significant events of his life. Entering the mills as a "learner" (at three cents an hour) in 1916 when he was eleven years old, he remained there until 1942, a period of twenty-six years. Except for a few months as a laborer with the Carolina Power and Light Company before his marriage in 1927, all these years were spent in cotton milling, solely in the Bladenboro Cotton Mills after 1923. After the war, he worked another seven years in the mills, making a total of thirty-three years in textiles compared to eighteen years in the shipyards. Most likely, it was the decades of the twenties and thirties that locked my father's memories so tenaciously into the culture of the mills. These were his most impressionable years—first as a farm youth moving into the radically different world of machines and village living, and then marriage and the years when growing responsibilities involving children and family made life more intense and memorable.

Furthermore, these were the decades when lifetime friendships were formed, friendships that he cherished and cultivated even after he left the mills. On weekend visits home from the Newport News shipyard, he circulated among friends and family members who continued to work in the Bladenboro mills. These were friends with whom he had shared years of common work experiences that bound them together as nothing else could. Tending the same machines day after day, month after month, year after year—all the while enduring the same frustrations of heat, noise, lint, short-time, low wages, supervisors—all these shared experiences created enduring friendships with the David James Paits, the Jetter Hesters, the Leland Shipmans, the Sam Edwardses, the Tully Singletarys, the Roy Davises, the John Paits, and a host of others, both men and women, whom my father treasured. Later, when he noted that his world was "gone," he was clearly thinking about the demise of the men and women with whom he had shared so much in the workplace, the villages, the church. His world of the mills, forged simultaneously in the crucible of common experiences at work, at home, and at worship, existed now only in his memory.

Another dimension of that lost world that persisted so tenaciously concerned life in the Old Mill village, where he had lived first with his parents and then throughout the early years of his marriage until 1934. Village living assured that his contacts with fellow workers did not end with the shift whistle because the houses were so closely situated. For example, while sitting on our front porch and looking across the street at the facing houses, one could easily see the homes of Bill Hester, Lon Deaver, Salon Ludlum, Tully Singletary, Fred Williams, and Rob Carter. And, of course, on our side of the street, there were houses to our right, left, and behind. The closeness resulted in an intimacy and commingling of working families that strengthened relationships made at work. Just as workers bonded from common experiences at work, their families similarly bonded as a consequence of shared experiences in village living. This was especially true when two families occupied the same house—as our family did on three occasions.

Dual occupancy was not uncommon in the Old and New Mill villages. Such tight living helped to produce a sense of community that work experiences elsewhere did not erase from my father's memory. Of course, his identification with village life was also partly caused by the existing class lines and the result of the social isolation of village residents from other segments of the surrounding community. Fortunately, today the barriers of class that once separated my father's generation of mill workers from others in the broader Bladenboro community have largely disappeared. Nevertheless, his memories of village living remain powerful and persistent. Although the villages, the physical symbols of his lost world, no longer exist, they clearly endure in the fabric of his mind.

It should be evident to readers of this book that the lost world that my father experienced was as much mine as his. That world largely shaped and molded my views of life before I entered military service in June 1951. During the thirteen years from 1929, the year of my birth in the Old Mill village, until 1942, when my father found employment in the Wilmington shipyard, our worlds were identical. These were the years when he ran the same set of intermediate frames in the New Mill, the years that substantially locked him mentally into our shared world—now gone—and that generated most of the memories that are the principal basis for this book.

My realization of our having shared a common world was strikingly confirmed when, years after her death in 1979, we visited the grave site of my mother. While in the cemetery, my father (then in his eighties) and I visited the headstones of people whom we both had known, he as a working adult and I as a youngster. As we stood and talked about experiences we had had with deceased workers from the mills and others from the town, to my surprise (although it shouldn't have been!), I discovered that we were discussing individual men and women who had played important roles not only in his life but in mine. In this cemetery and another half-dozen around Bladenboro were scores of friends who had tremendously influenced us in countless ways. Many of them had lived in the mill villages and spent their lives running the cards, the slubbers, the speeders, the intermediates, the twisters, the winders, the warps, and the spinning frames that composed the visible, physical dimension of the world my father perceived to be gone. However, it was the intangible world of lost relationships, the human dimension, emanating principally from his working in the mills and our life in the village, the haunting ghosts of men and women now deceased, that we then missed and reminisced about so nostalgically. The memory of them reflected a world that now existed only in our minds and the minds of others who, like us, had lived and worked at least part of their lives in the villages and works of the Bladenboro Cotton Mills during the thirties and forties. This thriving company with its throbbing village life was gone forever; however, it had left in its wake a residual world of memories that formed the very essence of who we then were.

My journey through and exit from the world that produced the memories recorded here was less traumatic than that experienced by many of my contemporaries born in the villages. As previously noted, my mother, whose father was both a small landowner and the owner of a sawmill, absolutely rejected the notion that her children were destined to work in cotton mills. Although nearly all her maternal aunts, uncles, and cousins (the Hesters) worked in the mills and some lived in the villages (the same was partly true for my father's siblings), her expectations for her two sons went much beyond life there. In her view, the escalator to something different and better was education. It was the means to a better life. Although she firmly believed that there was nothing shameful about work in the mills (it was honest work, and her husband and relatives worked there), she believed that one should do better if it were possible to do so. Consequently, with the strong support of my father, who felt the same as she about education, she enrolled me in the preschools available in the Old Mill village in the early thirties. After I entered the public schools, when her health permitted she aggressively monitored my progress in the elementary grades to make certain that I tracked with the top students, who were always taught by the best teachers. As a result, my child-hood associations crossed class lines. I developed permanent and cherished friendships with classmates from the surrounding farm and Front Street homes as well as those from the mill villages.

In my growing-up years, my mother was strong in religious faith and full of sound advice. "Get an education," she drummed into my head. "It's the one thing that nobody can ever take from you." To counter the class distinctions that she knew existed in the schools, she advised: "You just remember, son. You're no better than anybody in that school, but you're just as good—and don't you forget it!" And she was optimistic and clairvoyant about the future. "You've got to be prepared for opportunities," she often said. "You never know what might turn up, and you've got to be ready or you'll miss out." As I advanced toward high school graduation, my parents' obvious pride in my achievements, how-ever small, made it difficult for me to disappoint them. Thus the journey away from the mills was made easier by parents whose love and encouragement pushed me forward and filled me with an ambition to be a "somebody." Simultaneously moving with me through the schools to graduation were several classmates whose parents also worked in the mills and who, like my parents, wanted a better life for their children. We were more fortunate than our classmates from the villages who lacked the strong parental sup-port we enjoyed.

My mother was right about the opportunities that the postwar years were to offer to those who were ready. Although filled with uncertainties, the times were hopeful and expectant as thousands of returning veterans, exploiting the G.I. Bill, entered colleges and universities. Graduating from high school in 1947 with no financial means for college, I was unexpectedly rescued by Uncle Artie, who provided a gift of four hundred dollars for my first year's tuition at Wake Forest University, and by W. A. Hough, my high school principal, who arranged a job at hashing (serving and waiting on tables) so I could pay for my room and board. Borrowed money and work saw me through the second year. These were tremendously mind-broadening years under truly great teachers.

Financially unable to return to Wake Forest for my junior year in 1949 and unwilling to have my parents mortgage their small home by White Oak Original Free Will Baptist Church so that I might do so, I was rescued again—this time by Robert Randall, one of my former high school teachers who was now a principal of Williams Township School in Columbus County, North Carolina. Randall desperately needed a seventh-grade teacher and offered me the position, taking a chance that a promising nineteen-year-old former student could and would do the job well. I reluctantly accepted the position and discovered the importance of teaching. The discovery changed my life forever.

Two years at Williams Township were followed by two years of military service that entitled me to the Korean G.I. Bill. In 1953 I transferred to the University of Colorado at Boulder, where I used the G.I. benefits to earn the B.A. and M.A. degrees in history. Returning to teaching in 1955, for five years I taught American history and economics at Central and Geringer High Schools in Charlotte, North Carolina. My mother's dream that I would escape the mills had become a reality.

The journey from the mills, however, had not ended, although my distance from the preschool in the Old Mill village kept increasing. Now married to a teacher, who felt as strongly about education as my mother, I was ever encouraged by Virginia to exploit the opportunities that continued to arise. While teaching in Charlotte in 1959, I was awarded a John Hay Whitney Foundation Fellowship in the Humanities to attend Northwestern University, where I spent a year monitoring courses and reading broadly in the humanities, all of which was informed by my knowledge of the workaday life of mill hands and their families. More than ever I was aware of the tremendous distance—not just physical distance—that lay between the Old Mill village, where I was born into a culture of limited expectations, and the challenging culture of the intellectual world of great scholars who were then at Northwestern. The Northwestern experience convinced me to follow the advice of Hal Bridges and Robert Athearn, outstanding scholars at the University of Colorado, Boulder, and enroll in the doctoral program there. The research seminars of Bridges, Athearn, and others strongly enhanced my interest in labor history (which at that time was not a major field of graduate study) and led to a dissertation involving labor-management conflict in Colorado and the Rocky Mountain West. I was awarded the Ph.D. degree in history in 1964.

Afterward I accepted a teaching position at Southeast Missouri State University, where I taught until retirement—thirty-one years. Although the university was situated in a rural setting away from such industrial centers as St. Louis, my interest in labor persisted and was the focus of my teaching and publication career. And the opportunities to journey farther away from the Old Mill village continued. In 1980 I was awarded a National Endowment for the Humanities Resident Fellowship to explore the dimensions of the "new labor history" at Brown University, a year-long study directed by Joan Scott. As at Northwestern, my work at Brown again was influenced and informed by my firsthand knowledge of the everyday lives of working mill hands and their employers. From them I had gleaned humanistic perspectives about the working class that I otherwise would not have had. Paradoxically, in retrospect it seems that as educational opportunities apparently increased my distance away from the Old Mill village, I found that distance becoming increasingly shorter in terms of empathizing with and understanding the lives of men and women who had lived in the village in the thirties and forties.

In April 2001, I returned to Bladenboro for one of my frequent visits. My cousin Alma, whose family had occupied with my family a company house in the Old Mill village in the early thirties, had written that the New Mill of the Bladenboro Cotton Mills was being dismantled for salvage, its brick and heart lumber to be used elsewhere. I yearned for one last look at this industrial landmark. Since opening in 1923, this mill had been a workplace of my father, Alma's father, and hundreds of other men and women who ran its noisy machines. One afternoon, my wife and I drove my ninety-five-year-old father out to witness briefly the piece by piece removal of this vital remnant of local industrial history. Strangely

The destruction of the New Mill. The smokestack towers over the unseen Old Mill in the background (April 2001). Courtesy of the author.

and sadly, there were no mourners but us present. Occasionally, perhaps out of curiosity, a passerby drove slowly past on Highway 211 and looked at the destruction in progress. I recognized one of these spectators as Floyd Pait, an old playmate whose family had lived next door to us in the Old Mill village. I wondered what Floyd was thinking as he intently studied the machines at work on the mill, and whether he understood the significance of what was happening. After all, he, too, had been an inhabitant and an active worker in the cotton mill world that was now gone.

After I had walked about the project taking a series of pictures, deep in thought we sat on the roadside of Highway 211 and watched the men and machines busy dismantling the New Mill. A section of wall fronting the highway remained standing across from where we sat. My father suddenly pointed to the wall. "See that wall?" he asked. We indicated that we did. I anticipated immediately what he was about to say. "I run the same set of intermediates right behind that wall for thirteen years straight," he said with emotion. I also remembered his work behind the wall, for I had often taken his meals to him when he ran frames there. He then pointed to a certain bricked-in window. He related how in the thirties he had leaned out that very window many times for fresh air and how, when he did this in the springtime, he had longed so much to be back on the farm. Before we left the site, he noted that though times were hard then and uncertain, he had had some good times with friends in the New Mill. I sensed that he was thinking of men with whom he had worked, men like his brother-in-law David James Pait, Leland Shipman, Jetter Hester, and others who labored beside him in that part of the mill.

After the removal of the New Mill, only the Old Mill with its towering smokestack will remain of a once-thriving enterprise that provided employment for several generations of people in the southern part of Bladen County, North Carolina. The Old and New Mill villages are gone, Spinners' Field is gone, and the New Mill soon will be gone. Inevitably, like the death of the hundreds of workers who labored in the Bladenboro Cotton Mills, the Old Mill, the last visible evidence of the world my father cherished and

A roadside view of the destruction of the New Mill, showing the wall (right) behind which George G. Suggs, Sr., ran the same set of intermediate frames for thirteen years (April 2001). Courtesy of the author.

was so much a part of, will also be gone—to be replaced by who knows what. Will the replacement world be better? No one knows. But one can hope that it will be filled with people as courageous, determined, resilient, and durable as the ones who constituted the lost world that my father and I nostalgically remember. "My world is gone."

Suggested Additional Reading

Hall, Jacquelyn D., et al. *Like a Family: The Making of a Southern Cotton Mill World.* Fred W. Manson Series in Southern Studies. Chapel Hill: University of North Carolina Press, 1987.

Herring, Harriet L. *Welfare Work in Mill Villages: The Story of Extra-Mill Activities in North Carolina.* Social Studies Series. Chapel Hill: University of North Carolina Press, 1929; New York: Arno Press, 1971.

———. *Passing of the Mill Village: Revolution in a Southern Institution.* Chapel Hill: University of North Carolina Press, 1949; Westport, Conn.: Greenwood Press, 1977.

Newby, I. A. *Plain Folk in the South: Social Change and Cultural Persistence, 1880–1915.* Baton Rouge: Louisiana State University Press, 1989.

Rhyne, Jennings J. *Some Cotton Mill Workers and Their Villages.* Chapel Hill: University of North Carolina Press, 1930.

Index